Peace Journalism in Times of War

PEACE JOURNALISM

IN TIMES OF WAR

Peace & Policy, Volume 13

Susan Dente Ross and Majid Tehranian,
editors

Routledge
Taylor & Francis Group
LONDON AND NEW YORK

First published 2009 by Transaction Publishers

Published 2017 by Routledge
2 Park Square, Milton Park, Abingdon, Oxon OX14 4RN
711 Third Avenue, New York, NY 10017, USA

Routledge is an imprint of the Taylor & Francis Group, an informa business

Copyright © 2009 by Taylor & Francis.

Library of Congress Catalog Number: 2008051226

Library of Congress Cataloging-in-Publication Data

Peace journalism in times of war / Susan Dente Ross and Majid Tehranian, editors.
    p. cm. -- (Peace and policy ; v. 13)
  Includes bibliographical references and index.
  ISBN 978-1-4128-1004-3 (alk. paper)
    1. War--Press coverage. 2. Social conflict--Press coverage. 3. Conflict management--Press coverage. 4. Mass media and war. 5. Journalism--Objectivity. 6. Lebanon War, 2006--Press coverage. I. Ross, Susan Dente. II. Tehranian, Majid.

PN4784.W37P425 2009
070.4'333--dc22

                                  2008051226

ISBN 13: 978-1-4128-1004-3 (pbk)

Contents

Resources on Peace Journalism

Preface

Majid Tehranian

The Toda Institute was established in 1996 when the world was shifting from the Cold War era to a new one. The terrorist attacks of September 11, 2001 defined a new era for us. The new era could be called the Age of Terrorism. The existence of a single superpower, namely the United States, combined with the fact that growing inequalities in the world continue unaddressed, has opened up the opportunity for the lesser powers to express themselves in unconventional ways. One result of this phenomenon is that advanced societies may close themselves up. The world may become less mobile and may divide itself along urban-rural, developed-underdeveloped, or rich-poor axes. Terrorism, as the weapon of the weak, will play a more visible role during this era. More realistically, however, the world in now divided among the nomadic, agrarian, commercial, industrial, and digital worlds. The conflicts among these five modes of life will continue. The challenge before us is not only to avoid a nuclear holocaust that could wipe out the human race from the face of the earth, but to find ways of promoting day to day peace the world over. Certainly the field of peace journalism has much to contribute to this endeavor, as a field that bridges the divides of the modern world. As with any endeavor of great importance, creating a culture of peace will be challenging. We must collaborate in innovative ways if we are to succeed. This volume is dedicated to our shared future.

Introduction

Susan Dente Ross

Amid the ongoing, and sometimes volatile, debate over the nature and potential of peace journalism (see, e.g., *Conflict & Communication Online*, 6(2), 2007), *Peace Journalism in Times of War* compiles the current work and visionary insights of some of the most prominent scholars in the field. Offering a number of significant empirical studies to develop foundational data for development of the discipline, this issue also broadens the purview and terrain of peace journalism to encompass examination of new communication media and to offer essays on both the effects and the content of communications. The contributors to this volume have worked as a loose collective, the Peace Journalism Group, under the benevolent umbrella of the Toda Institute for Global Peace and Policy Research, and we wish to express our profound gratitude for the visionary focus and ongoing support of the Toda Institute.

For the past half-decade, members of the team have worked independently and collaboratively to increase systematic understanding of the value of peace journalism/communication to civil society. With Majid Tehranian's wise leadership and encouragement, the group has contributed to a more complex articulation of the various frames of conflict coverage, a greater clarification of the non-physical (e.g., structural, systemic, and cultural) aspects of global violence, and the ongoing creation of institutions, programs and strategies for enhancing constructive peace communication that increases mutual understanding, cooperation, reconciliation and conflict transformation.

As Dov Shinar explains later in this volume, this and other scholarly work on peace journalism,

> has led to re-framing the understanding of conflict from terms of a tug-of-war between two parties in which one side's gain is the other's loss, to the terms of relationships between various sides; to consider the context, and the need to identify a range of stakeholders broader than the sides directly engaged in violent confrontation; to understand the distinction between stated demands and underlying objectives; to

identify voices working for creative and non-violent solutions, and ways to transform and transcend the lines of conflict.

In this special edition focused on peace journalism/communication, several of our authors contribute to a set of articles focused on news coverage of the 2006 war between Israel and Lebanon. Research from Hackett and Schroeder, Ross, and Shinar, and an essay by Mandelzis and Peleg provide complementary yet distinct views of how the press covered and affected this and other wars during 2006.

Opening the volume, Dov Shinar's study of coverage in Canadian and Israeli newspapers of the 2006 Lebanon war asks why there is not more peace journalism. His content analysis of stories published during the war by one popular Canadian and one popular Israeli newspaper indicates that peace journalism is overshadowed, but not entirely excluded, by a preponderance of war journalism reporting. Amid a predominant tendency toward war journalism, he finds that common aspects of the political culture of the two countries, and geographical and social proximity to conflict areas may increase professional emphasis on peace journalism. On the conceptual level, his conclusions support claims made by other scholars that Pierre Bourdieu's approach to journalism as an autonomous institutional system is more suitable than others to analyze peace journalism (Hackett, 2006) and that peace journalism should be analyzed in broader frameworks than those supplied by conflict studies, peace studies, and conflict resolution studies (Ross, 2006).

Following with a study of the 2006 Afghan and Hezbollah-Israeli wars, Robert Hackett and Birgitta Schroeder ask whether anyone actually practices peace journalism. They compile a wealth of data to support the claim that media are engaged participants, not detached observers, of conflict situations. Their content analysis of more than 500 articles from Canadian, U.S., Israeli, and al-Jazeera online and print news outlets concerning the two 2006 wars suggests that media employ both war and peace journalism precepts in ways that tend to escalate conflict.

The critical discourse analysis of the coverage of the 2006 Lebanon war by Susan Dente Ross reaches similar conclusions through its close scrutiny of the news coverage wave of the war by one major U.S. daily newspaper. Ross explores the ways in which variable reporting and narrative practices, which briefly adopt some peace journalism strategies, may actually increase the conflict escalation of the coverage and reify the strategic hegemonic goals of the United States and Israel. This in-depth study of the three-month wave of coverage of the 2006 summer war in Lebanon indicates that developments on the ground, including increasing voices of peace, were rapidly overshadowed by coverage focused on U.S. and Israeli elite voices. She suggests that media dependence on powerful officials as sources of news *and* interpretation poses a significant direct threat to peace journalism practices, and that inclusion of divergent voices of dissonance *en passant* serves not to advance the goals of peace journalism, but to justify existing war journalism as *objective* reporting.

In a related essay, Lea Mandelzis and Samuel Peleg examine coverage of the 2006 Lebanon war as an example of the ability of the news, and newsmakers, to engage in "media manipulation" that directs or displaces audience attention to or from on-the-ground events. The two scholars suggest that news reporting ambiguously employs "security" (and insecurity) to strategically replace divisive feelings such as dismay, defiance, and depression with unifying emotions such as anxiety and uncertainty. They argue that Israeli-written media reports employed a gradual and progressive diversion process to shift audience attention away from military stalemates and battle casualties in Lebanon to emerging worldwide threats and admonitions from Teheran. They assert the media shifts from one topic to another, one geographical site to another, and one emotional manipulation to another are components of the diversion process through which Israeli media served Israeli national and military goals and initiatives.

Broadening our examination of war and peace communication beyond news coverage to encompass newer, entertainment media, Rune Ottosen investigates how concepts of peace communication apply within the environment of conflict-rife video games. Outlining processes through which the development costs of expensive simulators for training military personnel are defrayed through commercialization, including the spin-off of video war games from U.S. military projects, Ottosen uncovers the massive influence of the global military industrial complex upon the "games" our children play.

Qualitative research by Annabel McGoldrick complements Ottosen's empirical study with a discussion of the personal and social effects of conflict-rife communication. Also extending this volume beyond the confines of news media, McGoldrick draws on the fields of cognition and psychology to apply concepts from reception theory and psychotherapy to the content of in-depth interviews about televised violence. She employs a quasi-experimental design in which participants view either peace journalism or war journalism coverage of violent incidents to illicit the participant commentary upon which she builds her rich account of the diverse emotional and psychic effects of depictions of violence.

In the final study of this volume, Jake Lynch focuses on a different geographical front in the contemporary "War on Terrorism," the Philippines, to compare reporting of political violence in international media, on the one hand, with coverage in the country's own biggest daily newspaper, the *Philippine Daily Inquirer* (*PDI*), on the other. Designed to elicit evidence of "active peace journalism"—conscious efforts to counter war propaganda and create opportunities to consider and to value non-violent alternative responses to conflict—the study examines 368 articles over a period of a month from the point in June 2006 when Philippines armed forces were ordered to eradicate a group of armed rebels. The study found a higher proportion of active peace journalism in the *PDI* than in international media, despite the proximity of the *PDI* to the conflicts under discussion. Lynch suggests this finding, contrary to prior theorizing, may be partly accounted for by the media representation of the actions of the Philippines military as part of the U.S.-led "War on Terrorism," a linkage that called up the country's ambivalent relationship with the United States and provided opportunities for divergence from the anticipated war journalism.

As evident in this brief summary, the content of *Peace Journalism in Times of War* expands and deepens our empirical knowledge of the nature and effects of communicating conflict and underscores how much work remains to be done to increase the number of communicators and the breadth of communications that improve, rather than impede, the quality of individual and collective life. To assist other researchers in this important endeavor, we complete this volume with a focused bibliography of our recent contributions in the field of peace, conflict and communication. We invite you to join us in building on and from this literature to improve our understanding of this field and to move us toward a more just, equitable and peaceful world. And we thank the Toda Institute for Global Peace and Policy Research for its continued commitment to this team of scholars and to worldwide initiatives to increase global peace. Pax.

Susan Dente Ross
Moscow, Idaho, USA
January 2008

Why Not More Peace Journalism?
The Coverage of the 2006 Lebanon War in Canadian and Israeli Media[1]

Dov Shinar

Introduction

Peace journalism came to the world in the 1970s as a slogan and a set of ideas pioneered and developed by Norwegian scholar Johan Galtung in order to criticize the preference given by mainstream journalism around the world to war, violence, and propaganda, to causes promoted by elites and establishments, and to simple and polarized victory/defeat reality constructions. Advocating a change of attitudes and behaviors in the coverage and framing of war and peace, Galtung's concepts developed within some three decades into a philosophical framework and an arsenal of professional techniques (Lynch and McGoldrick, 2005). During most of this period, much of the writings on peace journalism consisted mostly of ideological claims, professional criticism and anecdotal discourse rather than factual knowledge.

The present comparative study of Canadian and Israeli media coverage of the 2006 Lebanon War is part of an ongoing effort to add a scholarly empirical dimension to the development of peace journalism. The study joins a trend of systematic field research that has emerged in recent years in the area, including the work of Ting Lee and Maslog (2005) and of the peace journalism international research group that has been active under the auspices of the Toda Institute for Global Peace and Policy Research (*Conflict & Communication Online* [CCO] 4(2), 2005; 5(2) 2006; 6(1) 2007).

War Journalism and Peace Journalism

Another purpose of the study is to make a conceptual contribution to adapting Galtung's model to twenty-first-century scholarly and professional terms. His dichotomous formula (1998) has considered traditional war coverage and framing from the perspective of a sports journalism model focused on winning in a zero-sum game, whereas peace journalism has been envisioned closer to a health reporting metaphor. Rather than using the sports-inspired victory/defeat formula, the health reporting metaphor can go beyond a patient's battle against the disease, so as to inform media consumers about the causes of the disease, and the full range of cures and preventive measures. This is clarified in Galtung's famous table.

In addition to their recognized merits, Galtung's concepts have become a topic of academic and professional controversy.

Critical allegations have been made against the destructive influence of peace journalism on cherished values of Western journalism, such as objectivity; against Galtung's problematic dichotomy between truth and propaganda; against the premise that every conflict must have a solution; against contradictions between peace journalism and established theories of mass communication; and on the need for a significant empirical basis to support the validity of the model (McGoldrick, 2006; Hanitzsch, 2004 a, b, 2007; Lynch, Peleg, and Loyne, 2007; Shinar, 2003, 2007). Peace journalism has been growing conceptually and professionally, as shown by Becker (1982); Hackett and Gruneau (2000); Höijer, Nohrstedt and Ottosen (2002); Bläsi (2004), and others. Galtung's original dichotomy has developed into more complex structures of competing types of framing in the coverage of conflict, and into strategies that aim at improving media representations and critical awareness (Knightley, 2000; Kempf, 2003; Lynch and McGoldrick, 2005).

This has led to reframing the understanding of conflict from terms of a tug-of-war between two parties in which one side's gain is the other's loss, to the terms of relationships between various sides; to consider the context, and the need to identify a range of stakeholders broader than the sides directly engaged in violent confrontation; to understand the distinction between stated demands and underlying objectives; to identify voices working for creative and non-violent solutions, and ways to transform and transcend the lines of conflict. Also peace journalism has raised the awareness of conflict beyond the direct physical violence typical of war journalism coverage to encompass underlying structural and cultural violence.

The relevance of peace journalism lies in its contribution to the effective presentation of issues of global significance to media professionals and to the public. Through its democratic orientation, peace journalism is expected to enhance public awareness, and encourage the change of

PEACE/CONFLICT JOURNALISM	WAR/VIOLENCE JOURNALISM
I. PEACE/CONFLICT – ORIENTED Explore conflict formation, x parties, y goals, and z issues. General win/win orientation. Open space, open time; causes and outcomes anywhere, also in history/culture. Making conflicts transparent. Giving voice to all parties; empathy, understanding. See conflict/war as a problem, focus on conflict creativity. Humanization of all sides; more so the worse the weapons. Proactive: prevention before any violence/war occurs. Focus on invisible effects of violence (trauma and glory, damage to structure/culture).	I. WAR/VIOLENCE – ORIENTED Focus on conflict arena, 2 parties, 1 goal (win), war general zero sum orientation. Closed space, closed time; causes and exits in arena, who threw the first stone. Making wars opaque/secret. "Us—them" journalism, propaganda, voice, for "us." Sees "them" as the problem, focus on who prevails in war. Dehumanization of "them"; more so the worse the weapons. Reactive: waiting for violence before reporting. Focus only on visible effect of violence (killed, wounded and material damage).
II. TRUTH – ORIENTED Expose untruths on all sides/uncover all cover-ups.	II. PROPAGANDA – ORIENTED Expose "their" untruths/help "our" cover-ups/lies.
III. PEOPLE – ORIENTED Focus on suffering all over; on women, aged, children, giving voice to the voiceless. Give name to all evil-doers. Focus on people peacemakers.	III. ELITE – ORIENTED Focus on "our" suffering; on able-bodied elite males, being their mouthpiece. Give name of their evil-doer. Focus on elite peacemakers.
IV. SOLUTION – ORIENTED Peace = nonviolence + creativity. Highlight peace initiatives, also prevent more war. Focus on structure, culture, the peaceful society. Aftermath: resolution, reconstruction, reconciliation.	IV. VICTORY – ORIENTED Peace = victory = ceasefire Conceal peace-initiative, before victory is at hand. Focus on treaty, institution, and the controlled society. Leaving for another war, return when the old fires flare up.

attitudes and behaviors related to the understanding of global, regional and local governance in all worlds. Experience leads us to think that the adoption of peace journalism can help delineate the potential global impact of conflicts, call public attention and opinion to such threats; indicate and hopefully satisfy demands for more balanced coverage; and stimulate alternative interpretations and critical reflection.

The War

It is no easy task to provide background comments on any war in studies dealing with critical approaches to media war coverage, particularly peace journalism. In the absence of direct access to the actual field of operations or to reliable sources, most such comments in research reports are based on secondary analyses of information selected from the media. This introduces a permanent risk of falling into the very traps criticized in the mainstream coverage, such as the media tendency to focus on simple decontextualized events and to avoid analyses of complex processes, to emphasize zero-sum-game approaches and sports-like journalism, to present "us vs. them" scenarios, and to mobilize behind elite positions. This risk is particularly true in deeply ingrained ethnic, nationalist, ideological, and religious conflicts such as the one known in the West as the 2006 Lebanon War, in Lebanon as the July War, and in Israel as the Second Lebanon War.

Nevertheless, it seems possible to present some basic facts about the war, carefully selected from a variety of sources, including but not limited to Canadian, Israeli, and Arabic, so as to present necessary background information, while reducing the dangers inherent in the nature of the coverage.

The present analysis concerns the coverage of the war activities in Lebanon and Israel during 34 days between July 12 and August 14, 2007. The general background is the history of war between Israel and the Lebanese army in 1948: occasional clashes of different military and political natures with Arab forces based in southern Lebanon; the Palestine Liberation Organization between the mid-1970s and the early 1980s and Hezbollah since then; a full-scale Israeli military invasion of Lebanon in 1982; the IDF (Israel Defense Forces, the official name of the Israeli army) presence in what the West and Israel consider a "security zone" in southern Lebanon for 19 years; and a unilateral Israeli withdrawal in 2000.

The 2006 war started when a Lebanese Hezbollah unit launched a surprise attack across the Israeli border killing eight Israeli soldiers and capturing two. Almost immediately, Israel sent an armored force into southern Lebanon, followed by massive air raids against Hezbollah positions, some of them located in civilian areas in Shiite suburbs of Beirut and other parts of Lebanon, wrecking Lebanon's economy, destroying its infrastructure, and inflaming political passions. At the same time, Hezbollah rained thousands of Katyusha rockets and longer-range missiles on military and civilian targets in northern Israel, including the densely populated port city of Haifa.[2]

In addition to daily air attacks on Hezbollah military positions, and Lebanese civilian targets, in the final three days of the war Israel launched a ground invasion of southern Lebanon. The unsuccessful invasion did not produce the strategic results hoped for by Israel and the United States, and helped Hezbollah to maintain a victorious image.[3]

On August 11, 2007, the United Nations Security Council unanimously adopted Resolution 1701 (approved later by the Israeli and Lebanese governments) that called for the end to the fighting, for the disarmament of Hezbollah, for Israel's withdrawal from Lebanon, and for the deployment of Lebanese and UNIFIL (United Nations Interim Force in Lebanon) troops in southern Lebanon. *The war came to its official end at 8 a.m. on August 14, when the U.N.-imposed cease-fire went into effect.*[4]

At that time, Israel's Ministry of Foreign Affairs reported that 162 Israelis had been killed during the war—43 civilians and 119 soldiers. Lebanon's Higher Relief Council estimated that 845 Lebanese had been killed—743 civilians, 34 soldiers and 68 Hezbollah fighters. Hezbollah provided no official estimates of its own losses, but Israel estimated that it had killed 500-600 guerrilla fighters.[5]

The Questions Explored

The comparison between the coverage of the 2006 Lebanon War in the Israeli and Canadian press seeks to answer questions such as:

1. To what extent does the coverage of the 2006 Lebanon War by Canadian and Israeli media display war journalism and peace journalism framing?
2. Do coverage patterns reflect shared ideologies? More specifically, research on the first Gulf War reveals that the media in countries that share similar political and economic ideologies covered that war in similar, though not necessarily identical terms (Kaid, Harville, Ballotti and Wawrzyniak, 1993). Notwithstanding differences in size, structure and climate, do the ideological, political and economic similarities between Canada and Israel produce the same or similar framing and patterns of conflict coverage?
3. Or, does different geographic proximity more directly explain coverage patterns? Does the direct involvement of the Israeli media in the conflict make it more inclined toward war journalism while Canadian media coverage reflects theory that distance enables journalists to show a stronger tendency towards peace journalism? Even though Canada's international peacemaker/peacekeeper image and policies do not detach it entirely from the conflict, and Canadian Jewish and Arab communities show interest and concern over Middle Eastern affairs, does Canada's geographic remove from the conflict area increase its peace journalism coverage?

Coding Protocol and Method

This study is a content analysis of stories published on and during the 2006 Lebanon War by Canadian and Israeli printed and online popular media. Included in our sample are two typical tabloids—*Yediot Aharonot* (printed edition) in Israel and the *Toronto Sun* (online edition) in

Canada. *Yediot Aharonot* (*YA*) enjoys the highest circulation among all Israeli newspapers: about 40 percent of the Israeli Jewish population on weekdays (some 380,000 copies) and more than 50 percent on weekends (estimated at some 680,000 copies).[6] The *Toronto Sun* (*TS*) also enjoys a considerable circulation, estimated at some 200,000 copies in weekdays, and some 400,000 on Sundays.[7]

Coding of all items about the war was conducted for the newspaper issues published between July 13 and August 17, 2006. A total of 277 items were coded and analyzed, 158 from *YA*, all of them front page-items, including their continuation in the inner pages; and 119 items from the *TS*: all items about the war in all parts of the paper, to make up for the fewer references to the war on the front page. Three communication students performed the coding, featuring a 92 percent coders' rate of reliability. Galtung's criteria to define both war journalism and peace journalism (1986, 1998) are the ancestral source of inspiration for analyzing conflict coverage to the present day. Ting Lee and Maslog (2005) developed his typology into thirteen indicators of war journalism and thirteen indicators of peace journalism that dominate the narrative. The present study borrowed ten of these criteria:

For War Journalism:

1. Marked visibility of war effects;
2. Emphasis on elite and official sources;
3. Conflict outcomes focused on war options;
4. Emphasis on "here and now" events;
5. Frequent good/bad tagging;
6. One or two-parties framing preferences;
7. Partisanship;
8. Zero-sum victory-defeat orientation (sports-coverage approach);
9. Victimizing language; and
10. Military vocabulary.

For Peace Journalism:

1. Less marked visibility of war effects;
2. Emphasis on "people sources";
3. Conflict outcomes focused on negotiation and agreement;
4. Emphasis on longer term processes and wider aspects;
5. Absence of good/bad tagging;
6. Multi-party framing preference;
7. No partisanship;
8. Win-win orientation (health-coverage approach);
9. Absence of victimizing language; and
10. Absence of military vocabulary.

These criteria served to code, tabulate, test for chi-square significance levels, and index the data with each analyzed item categorized according to its dominant war, or peace, journalism frame. Indexes were produced to classify a story as oriented toward war journalism or peace journalism, and composite means were calculated for each of these orientations, with scores given to each of these criteria, ranging from 1 (lowest) to 10 (highest).

General Findings: Dominant Frame— War Journalism Is Prevalent

The raw frequencies computed for all 277 items analyzed in the *YA/TS* joint sample display a marked tendency towards war journalism. The findings are presented in four groups: results of the war, professional orientation (visual dimensions of the war), social orientation, and political orientation in the coverage. Table 1 summarizes this tendency.

Table 1
War Journalism and Peace Journalism Indicators in the total YA/TS sample
(Raw frequencies, percentages)*

War Journalism		Peace Journalism	
(n=277)			
%		%	
Expected Results			
1. Zero-sum orientation	37.5	Win-win orientation	44.0
2. War-oriented	50.9	Agreement-oriented	8.3
Professional Orientation: Visual Presentation			
3. Visible effects of war	67.9	Less visible effects of war	5.1
Social Orientation			
4. Elite/official sources	50.2	People-oriented sources	31.4
5. Uses victimizing language	50.1	Less victimizing language	48.4
6. Uses military discourse	36.1	Less military discourse	58.8
Political Orientation			
7. Partisan	52.0	Non-partisan	32.1
8. Good-bad tagging	64.3	No good and bad tagging	22.7
9. One/Two-party orientation	76.7	Multi-party orientation	5.4
10. Focus here and now	68.2	Wider aspects of conflict	6.1

* These percentages add up to less than 100% because they do not include categories such as "other," "unclear," "missing data," counted in the original tables.

A general tendency toward war journalism appears in most criteria. In the professional area, expressed by the volume of visual display, more than three-fourths of all items show visible effects of the war, while only 5.1 percent do not display such effects.

Social Orientation

The social orientation of the coverage reveals that more than 50 percent of the items rely on elite/official sources, while less than one-third of them rely on "people-sources." On the other hand, the use of victimizing and non-victimizing language is almost identical, and only some one-third of the items display military vocabulary, while almost 60 percent do not.

Political Orientation

The political orientation of the coverage shows that about one-half of items reveal a partisan orientation; about two-thirds display a clear good/bad tagging and three-quarters display a one- or two-sided orientation. About one-fifth of the items do not show good/bad tagging, and only some 5 percent show a multi-party orientation.

Other War Journalism Traits

In addition, more than two-thirds of the items relate to "here-and-now," while only some 6 percent relate to wider contexts. Insofar as the expected results of the war are concerned, a zero-sum orientation (winning/losing) could be expected, but contrary to expectations this is not clear in the coverage. More than one-third of the items display this orientation, but 44 percent do not. On the other hand, the raw frequencies show that options oriented towards war are present in more than half of the items and absent in 8.3 percent of them.

This general tendency towards war journalism is confirmed by the composite mean indexes computed from the aggregation of the 1-10 grades assigned to each item. *TS* earned a 7.78 mean index while *YA* reached a 6.75 index. The mean indexes for peace journalism are 1.46 for *YA*, and 1.82 for the TS. Together with the raw frequencies, these mean indexes indicate a tendency towards war journalism that leads one to look more closely at comparative results for the Canadian and the Israeli newspapers.

Comparative Findings

The frequencies computed for the 158 items analyzed in *YA*, compared with the 119 items analyzed in the *TS*, display more varied tendencies than the raw frequencies and the composite indexes. War journalism framing is considerable in both newspapers, but the differences in emphases and in the use of peace journalism framing allow us to answer the questions above in more decisive and specific terms.

Expected Results of the War

This group of indicators refers to the variables that reflect the results of the war expected by the newspapers. The more the coverage displays a sports-like, zero-sum game orientation, and the more war is the dominant frame of reference, the more a newspaper displays a tendency towards war journalism. The more the coverage displays a health-coverage-like, win-win orientation, and the more negotiations and agreement are the dominant frame of reference, the more a newspaper displays a tendency towards peace journalism. Examples include citations such as:

> The incident is shaping up to be a major international embarrassment for Israeli leaders, who have vehemently denied targeting the post (*TS*, July 27, 2006, p. 7).

> Olmert: We will win but the price will be awful (*YA*, August 8, 2006, p. 1).

> U.N. security council envoys yesterday put the finishing touches on a draft resolution from France and the United States calling for a halt to fighting between Israel and Hezbollah guerrillas and setting terms for a settlement to the conflict (*TS*, August 7, 2006, p. 36).

YA is more adamant in its zero-sum orientation, while the win-win orientation is more marked in *TS*. On the other hand, the *TS* presents an expectation of war-oriented results (about two-thirds of the items) much more than *YA* (about one-third).

Professional Orientation: Visual Dimensions of the War

This indicator refers to the volume of the visual coverage through the use of discursive or pictorial images. Previous research indicates that the more marked the volume of visual material, the stronger the tendency towards war journalism. The following citations clarify this indicator:

> A military vehicle crosses a damaged bridge south of Beirut that was attacked by Israeli warplanes during the month-long conflict in Lebanon (*TS*, August 16, 2006, p. 9).

> During many years, Israel's civilian sector has not known such an attack... One hundred Katyousha rockets fell in the North, 115 civilians hurt, 2 killed ... frightened families started to abandon their homes... A Katyousha rocket hit Haifa, bombing of strategic facilities in Haifa Bay will cause a disaster... IDF attacked hundreds of targets in Lebanon and imposed a blockade on the country, 50 Lebanese killed... Target: Hezbollah neighborhood south of Beirut (*YA*, July 14, 2006, p. 1).

On the other hand, less emphasis on the visible effects of the war are indicated by citations such as these:

One girl in two wars—three times a week Bat-Sheva Nail goes from Kyriat Shmona to Naharia for regular dialysis treatment. Before the war she dreamed of a kidney transplant, now she dreams of a quiet week in Eilat (*YA*, August 9, 2006, p. 15).

Oil: long term pain, but prices should drop ... (*TS*, July 29, 2006, p. 33).

YA's visual treatment of the conflict is more clearly war-oriented than *TS*'s. The volume of visible effects of the war is significantly higher and that of less visible effects is relatively lower in the Israeli newspaper. Also, *YA* shows more photos. Slightly more than 60 percent of the items in *YA* showed photos obtained from local photographers, as compared with 7.6 in *TS* (Tables 3 and 3A). Albeit less significant than other findings, this might result from the ability of the Israeli paper to deploy more in-house staff than the Canadian daily.

Social Orientation

This group of indicators refers to variables that reflect the self-positioning and the social perception of the newspapers. The more the coverage relies on elite and official sources, the more it displays a tendency towards war journalism. The more the coverage relies on "people-sources," the more it tends toward peace journalism. Also war journalism uses victimizing language and military discourse more than peace journalism. Examples of the differences follow.

Citations emphasizing elite/official sources:

World condemns, leaders denounce Israel over killing 56 civilians (*TS*, July 31, 2006, p. 5).

Olmert and Peretz follow military attacks on a Northern front position, PM: the entire world is checking right now if we bend down—and this will not happen; Nassrallah hides in an underground bunker, Hiazbollah neighborhood in Beirut destroyed in IAF bombings (*YA*, July 16, 2006, p. 1).

Citations emphasizing people sources:

Wife: Israeli attack on U.N. site not accidental (*TS*, July, 28, 2006, p. 4).

Katyousha rocket lands inside living room, five kids hurt. Zion Mor cried bitterly trying to understand how in one moment his wife and five kids were hit last night in Zefat (*YA*, July 14, 2006, pp. 1, 5).

Citations emphasizing victimizing language:

Every day becomes worse in Lebanon (*YA*, July 20, 2006, p. 16).

There are victims on all sides: those in Israel are obliged to live in shelters, as well as the great multitude of Lebanese, who once more, see their country being destroyed (*TS*, August 6, 2006, p. C6).

Table 2
War Journalism (WJ) and Peace Journalism (PJ) Indicators
Expected Results of the War

(Percentages, chi square significance tests)

	YA	TS	Total	Chi-sq. Sign. level
	N= 158 % of items in each newspaper	N= 119 % of items on topic		
Zero-sum vs. Win-win orientation				0.000
Zero-sum	44.9	27.7	37.5	
Win-win	24.7	69.7	44.0	
Option-Orientation				0.000
War-oriented (WJ)	36.7	69.7	50.9	
Agreement-oriented (PJ)	5.1	12.6	8.3	

Table 3
War Journalism (WJ) and Peace Journalism (PJ) Indicators
Professional Orientation (Visual Presentation)

(Percentages, chi square significance tests)

	YA	TS	Total
	N= 158	N= 119	
Visibility of effects of war	% of items in each newspaper		% of items on topic
Yes (WJ)	73.4	60.5	67.9
No (PJ)	6.3	3.4	5.1

Chi-square significance level = 0.000

Table 3A
War Journalism (WJ) and Peace Journalism (PJ) Indicators
Visual Presentation (Photos)

(Percentages, chi square significance tests)

	YA	TS	Total	Chi-sq. Sign. level
	N= 158 % of items in each	N= 119 newspaper	% of items on topic	
Photos added?				0.008
Yes (WJ)	64.6	53.8	59.9	
No (PJ)	31.6	46.2	37.9	
Photographers Identity				0.000
Local	60.2	7.6	32.6	
News agency	29.6	27.7	28.6	

> Venezuelan president Hugo Chavez renewed his criticism of Israel's military offensive in Lebanon, calling it a "new Holocaust." Israel has gone mad, Chavez said in his weekly broadcast Sunday. They are massacring children, and no one knows how many are buried (*TS*, August 8, 2006, p. 4).

Although both newspapers show a clear preference for elite/official sources, this tendency is more marked in *YA*. The lack of people-oriented sources is also more marked in the Israeli newspaper. In both cases, these percentages are higher than the total distribution and there is a significant level of chi-square dependency. Also military discourse is significantly more characteristic of *YA*, while victimizing language is significantly more typical of the *TS*.

Political Orientation

This group of indicators refers to the variables that reflect or suggest the political position of the newspapers. The more partisan the coverage, the more it uses tagging toward one or more sides. The more it emphasizes one or two parties to the conflict, and the more it focuses "here-and-now," the more it displays a tendency towards war journalism. The less partisan, less tagging, and the more emphasis on a multiple-party orientation and a wider range of aspects in the conflict, the more it tends toward peace journalism. Examples follow:

Citations showing partisanship:

> Israel and the world against Hezbollah criminals... Hezbollah is the attacker ... it is about time to uproot the myth that it is impossible to win over Hezbollah's "guerilla fighters." The IDF can and is winning (*YA*, August 12, p. 1).

Citations showing tagging of good/bad:

> Bombs continued to drop and Israeli ground forces moved deeper into Lebanon as MacKay insisted that the choice between a democratic state and a terrorist organization was simple. He minced no words in characterizing Hezbollah as "a cancer" and a "group of cold-blooded killers" while vigorously supporting PM Stephen Harper's view that Israeli response was "measured" (*TS*, August 2, 2006, p. 20).

> A large group of the *Egoz* crack unit entered last Thursday into Marun-a-Ras, determined to purify it from its Katyousha missiles launching base. But the battle went wrong and five of them were killed... An IDF official source: the event will be investigated but the troops deserve to be decorated (*YA*, July 23, 2006, p. 5).

Citations showing one- or two-party orientation:

> Israel has said it will not pull put around 10,000 troops in the south until a strengthened international force is deployed. Lebanese health minister Mohammad Kalifeh said the war has killed 925 people, mostly civilians... The toll did not include yesterday's casualties. About one-third of the dead were under the age of 13, he said (*TS*, August 8, 2006, p. 4).

Table 4
War Journalism (WJ) and Peace Journalism (PJ) Indicators
Social Orientation

(Percentages, chi square significance tests)

	YA	TS	Total	Chi-sq. Sign. level
	N= 158	N= 119		
	% of items in each newspaper	% of items on topic		
Source Orientation				
Elite/Official Sources (WJ)	56.3	42.0	50.2	0.000
People Oriented Sources (PJ)	29.1	34.5	31.4	
Language				0.000
Victimizing (WJ)	32.9	73.1	50.1	
Non victimizing (PJ)	64.6	26.9	48.4	
Who are the victims?				0.000
Lebanese	1.9	50.4	22.7	
Israeli	29.7	10.1	21.3	
Both	1.3	12.6	6.1	
Not mentioned	64.6	26.9	48.4	
Military Discourse				0.000
Yes (WJ)	56.3	9.2	36.1	
No (PJ)	35.4	89.9	58.8	

"The media does not always show the right pictures," [Andy] Ram said. "What I see, they are showing mostly the Lebanese side and the damage Israel makes there. They don't show the 1.5 million people living underground in the north of Israel right now. We prefer to get news from our families, from the people living inside the situation" (TS, August 9, 2006, p. S2).

We should remember that there are losses in war, said yesterday a senior IDF officer after an officer and an armored unit soldier were killed in combat with Hezbollah (YA, July 25, 2006).

Citations showing multi-party orientation:

"World condemns, leaders denounce Israel over killing of 56 civilians" (TS, July 31, 2006, p. 5); "While Nassrallah was speaking, and two negotiators ... met in Beirut with Lebanon's PM and with the leader of the Shi'ite movement Amal, Nabi'l Berry, Chairman of Beirut's parliament" (YA, July 17, 2006, p. 8).

References to "here and now":

Table 5
War Journalism (WJ) and Peace Journalism (PJ) Indicators
Political Orientation

(Percentages, chi square significance tests)

	YA	TS	Total	Chi-sq. Sign. level
	N= 158 % of items in each newspaper	N= 119	% of items on topic	
Partisan vs. Non-Partisan Attitudes				0.000
Partisan (WJ)	23.4	56.3	37.6	
Non-Partisan (PJ)	48.7	43.7	47.4	
Tagging				0.000
Good-bad division (WJ)	63.9	64.7	63.4	
No tagging (PJ)	14.6	33.6	22.7	
One/Two-Party vs. Multiple-Party Orientation				0.000
One/Two-party orientation (WJ)	85.4	88.2	86.7	
Multiple-party orientation (PJ)	4.4		6.7	5.4
Focus "here and now" vs. wider aspects of conflict				0.000
Here and now (WJ)	79.1	53.8	68.2	
Wider aspects (PJ)	8.9	2.5	6.1	

Edict defends Hezbollah—A top Egyptian cleric issued an edict yesterday defending Hezbollah fight against Israel, as Arab support for the militant group grows (TS, July 30, 2006, p. 10).

Officials in the Northern command: The significant phase last night. Hezbollah's fighter's bodies will be transferred to Israeli territory to become negotiation chips, Intelligence commander: Hezbollah is hurt but not broken (YA, July 24, 2006, p. 1).

References to wider contexts and circumstances:

Israel's unilateral withdrawal from South Lebanon in 2000 showed a clear willingness to move toward a genuine, lasting peace. Yet Hezbollah and its sponsors, Iran and Syria instead interpreted it as weakness, to be exploited (TS, July, 29, 2006, p. 20).

During the recent few years, since the IDF withdrawal, the Israeli North and Lebanese South lick their wounds … during the last 25 years Hezbollah weighs carefully every step of its way. With no visible explanation, the militia is now leading itself and a large part of the Lebanese people into a suicidal campaign, perhaps the biggest in the history of the conflict in the Middle East (*YA*, July 17, 2006, p. 4).

TS is more partisan than non-partisan and than *YA* on this matter. On the other hand, some two-thirds of the items in both papers display a clear good/bad orientation, and more than 80 percent of the items in both newspapers display a one-party or two-party rather than a multiple-party orientation. In addition, both newspapers focus more on immediate aspects, with *YA* displaying a clearly more marked emphasis on the here and now.

Analyzing the Findings: Back to the Questions

The first of the three questions posed in this study is to what extent does the coverage of the 2006 Lebanon War by Canadian and Israeli media display war journalism and peace journalism framing? The combined analysis of all items in both newspapers (Table 1) indicates a general preference for war journalism. More than 50 percent of all items show this preference (with some war journalism variables featured in two-thirds to three-quarters of all items, with the exception of two indicators: the use of military discourse, and a zero-sum orientation). However, some variables indicate encouraging signs of the possibility that peace journalism is not totally disregarded. Thus, even though about half of the items indicate expectations that the war will result in more war, the win-win orientation as opposed to the sports coverage model is present in 44 percent of the items.

In addition, some 60 percent of the items do not feature military discourse. Together with the considerable percentage of items based on "people-oriented sources," and on "less victimizing language," this finding is encouraging in the sense that it suggests possible directions to strengthen the use of peace journalism in certain areas of conflict coverage.

The deconstruction of the coverage in both newspapers allows answering the second and third questions. The second question is to what extent does Canadian and Israeli press coverage produce the same or similar framing and patterns of conflict coverage in accord with their ideological, political, and economic similarities, regardless of differences in the nations' size, structure, and climate? The findings show that the tendency towards war journalism is common to the coverage of both newspapers.

Table 6 shows a composite picture of the preceding detailed tables, featuring commonalities in the professional area, where both emphasize the tendency to show visible effects of the war. The political orientation of the coverage is also similar in that a majority of the items in both newspapers focus on immediate events rather than on wider, processual aspects of the conflict, and show a one- or two-party rather than a multiple-party orientation. Also, most items in both newspapers feature the tagging of the parties in terms of good and bad (Table 4).

The extent of partisan attitudes is the only variable that does not show total compatibility. While both newspapers show non-partisan attitudes in general terms, more items in the *TS* show a stronger partisan attitude. Some "Canadian dimensions" of the war and resulting divergence in ideologies between the two nations may help explain this fact, at least in part. In the context of the large number of Canadian citizens of Arab and particularly Lebanese origin, the evacuation of Canadian citizens from Lebanon in the beginning of the war became a salient Canadian political and human issue. The *TS* was openly sympathetic towards the Canadian

Table 6
War Journalism and Peace Journalism Framing
Schematic Summary of Similarities and Differences among YA and TS

War Journalism Framing		Peace Journalism Framing	
(n=277)			
Expected Results			
1. Zero-sum orientation	YA	Win-/win orientation	TS
2. War-oriented	TS	Agreement-oriented	YA
Professional Orientation			
3. Visible effects of war	Both	Less visible effects of war	None
Social Orientation			
4. Elite/official sources	YA	People-oriented sources	TS
5. Uses victimizing language	TS	Less victimizing language	YA
6. Uses military discourse	YA	Less military discourse	TS
Political Orientation			
7. Partisan	TS	Non-partisan	Both
8. Good-bad tagging	Both	No good and bad tagging	None
9. One/Two-party orientation	Both	Multi-party orientation	--
10. Focus here and now	Both	Wider aspects of conflict	--

evacuees. This was expressed, firstly, in items on the human and logistic aspects of evacuation under fire; and on the entrance of Canadian troops into Hezbollah-controlled areas to rescue stranded Canadians (*TS*, July 25, 2006, p. 3).

Also the *TS* items gave voice to complaints against the performance of the Canadian government in the evacuation: its slow pace, the crowded vessels, and the danger involved in keeping Canadian citizens on Lebanese soil. These items and others regarding Canadian financial aid to Lebanon and the possible participation of Canadian troops in a UNIFIL contingent raised a clear partisan attitude about Canadian involvement in the action, sympathy toward the evacuees, and criticism against Israel, (*TS*, July 17, 2006, p. 8; July 19, 2006, p. 5; July 20, 2006, p. 4; July 21, 2006, pp. 2, 24; July 22, 2006, pp. 3, 5). The partisan tendency in the *TS* coverage is supported by its social orientation; it used more "people-oriented sources" and more victimizing language toward Lebanese victims, and toward victims from both sides, while *YA* used less victimizing language. Items displaying such language in the Israeli paper refer mostly to Israelis (Table 4).

Finally, our third question refers to the influence geographical distance might have on the coverage, in the sense that "the more a society is involved in the conflict itself and the closer it is to the conflict region (in historical, political, economic or ideological terms), distortions of the conflict perception will be stronger" (Kempf et al., 2000). The question here is, in fact, to what extent does physical proximity to the conflict and direct involvement in it make Israel more emphatic on war journalism? By the same token, to what extent does the geographical distance of Canada from the conflict area—even considering the interest and concern showed by the Canadian Jewish and Arab communities in Middle Eastern affairs—produce a stronger tendency towards peace journalism in the Canadian press? Some aspects of the coverage display differences that might be explained by differences in the geographical and social proximity to the conflict in addition to different professional constraints imposed by distance.

YA displays the effects of proximity in its tendency towards war journalism far more than its Canadian counterpart both in the long-run coverage of the conflict during recent years and in the coverage of the hostilities in the summer of 2006. Our data on the coverage of the 2006 Lebanon War reveal much more frequent use of civilian and military local sources and of Israeli reporters and photographers in *YA*, while the *TS* used mostly copy obtained from global news agencies. This might

Table 7
Sources of the 2006 Lebanon War Coverage

(Percentages, chi square significance tests)
N = 318*

	YA N= 158	TS N= 119	Total	Chi-sq. Sign. level
	% of items in each newspaper		% of items on topic	
Sources – general				
International	13.1	14.5	13.8	0.000
Arab	6.3	11.4		
	8.8			
Israeli	73.1	17.1	45.2	
Canadian	0	41.7	41.7	
Other	7.5	15.2	11.3	
Israeli Military Sources				0.000
Yes	29.2	3.2	16.3	
No	70.8	96.8	83.7	
Reporters Nationality				0.000
Local	95.6	31.1	67.9	
News Agency	0	58.0	24.9	
Other	0.6	10.9	5.1	

* N is larger than in the other tables because the newspapers used more than one source.

explain some of the stronger tendency towards war journalism in the Israeli newspaper (Table 7), such as its expectations of zero-sum results, and its use of elite/official sources, and of military discourse (Table 6). Given this pattern of coverage, *YA* readers are probably more familiar with war journalism framing. Such war orientation is compounded by the impact of the almost universal army service in Israel, which affects most social networks.

However, at least one instance has been documented about the impact of Canadian social proximity to the conflict. The militant partisan coverage in the *TS* of the evacuation of Canadian citizens under fire, and of the entrance of Canadian troops into Hezbollah-controlled areas to rescue stranded Canadians, its expressions of sympathy toward the evacuees, and its criticism against Israel (see page 19) steered the Canadian newspaper closer to the war journalism style. This indicates that the degree of physical and social proximity to conflict areas may be a promising topic for further research on the potential for peace journalism.

Conclusions

The environment in which war journalism thrives has been explored through various conceptual approaches. The analysis of three such frameworks (Hackett, 2006), indicates that 1) Herman's and Chomsky's propaganda model usefully highlights some ways whereby state and capital influence journalism, but its one-factor ideological bias leads it to artificial reductionism and functionalism; and, 2) the deconstructionist approach of Shoemaker and Reese's "hierarchy of influences" model helps to assess pressures for and against peace journalism, but, like the propaganda model, its "anatomic" nature equally leads it to reductionism, and obscures the coherence of journalism as a cultural practice and form of knowledge-production. To some extent, both models echo traditional dichotomous approaches that need to be adapted to twenty-first-century terms.

Pointing out the merits of these models—in criticizing war journalism, for example—Hackett suggests that Pierre Bourdieu's approach to journalism as a relatively autonomous institutional sphere, allows conceptual space for dealing with peace journalism both in terms of the structural influences of and on the news media and the potential agency and creativity of journalists. Supported by Bläsi (2004) and others, this perception of journalism—in multi-dimensional, less dichotomous, and less deterministic institutional terms, and featuring value-charged normative social, political and professional dimensions—is more compatible with the current "empiricist" trend in the study of peace journalism: the trend of deconstructing, evaluating, and reconstructing practices of journalistic coverage rather than adopting the fragmenting positions induced by the two former models and others like them.

Along similar lines, others criticize the long-standing imprecise ideological focus of conflict studies, peace studies, and conflict resolution studies as a sole basis for the development of peace journalism (Ross, 2006). The present study joins the call for increasing the variety of peace journalism conceptual foundations from exclusive reliance on conflict-oriented models. Additional conceptual bases might include professional training patterns; constraints that encourage reactive, nationalistic reporting; approaches that transcend the bonds of identity and enmity toward symbolic rapprochement, and more.

On the professional level, the current trend of producing empirical findings for the development of peace journalism indicates a new phase in the research of conflict coverage. This phase takes the scholarly and professional interest in this type of journalism "beyond square one," the initial phase characterized by exploratory efforts dominated by ideology, professional discourse, and anecdote. In this new phase, field researchers and students dissect peace journalism into factual dimensions and components, looking for ways to implement it. While the exploratory efforts have provided conceptual cornerstones for the development of the area, they can greatly benefit from the growing amount and quality of field research typical of this second phase. The dissection of war journalism and peace journalism concepts into measurable components allows for scrutiny of some cross-cultural aspects of conflict reporting, including the Canadian and Israeli coverage of the 2006 Lebanon War. These help to identify comparative markers and indicate topics where efforts to promote peace journalism might be applied.

In the context of these empirical efforts, the present study indicates both the salience and the resistance of war journalism, as well as opportunities and challenges for the promotion of peace journalism. The impediments and opportunities arise from similarities in the presence of embedded professional norms that are more resilient to cross-cultural differences, and therefore more universal than others, such as formats and images (Sabine, 2005). Professional values—such as the tendency to visualize conflict and the expectation of war-oriented conflict results—are variables that stimulate the adherence to war journalism. In that, they resemble findings by Bläsi (2004), Hanitzsch (2004 a, b), and Dimitrova and Stromback (2005), and indicate possible areas of intervention on behalf of peace journalism. Such similarities also apply to some political aspects found in the present study and supported by Ting Lee and Maslog (2005)—such as partisanship, one/two party terminology, and "here-and-now" attitudes—that are salient and resistant components of the adherence to war journalism.

The present study adds to this list the geographical and human proximity to areas of conflict as variables that might enhance war journalism and challenge efforts to promote peace journalism. On the other hand, the relatively similar political orientation of the newspapers in the present study does not confirm findings that political variables, such as *war* motives, evaluation of political leaders and discursive stereotypes are more culture-bound and less universal (Sabine, 2005). In addition, the study indicates the existence of some significant cross-cultural differences, such as access to the conflict scene and a larger photographic output that is usually enjoyed by local newspapers due to the work of local staff, rather than to copy supplied by news agencies. This is supported by similar findings in Dimitrova and Stromback's study on the framing of the Iraq War in the elite newspapers in Sweden and the United States (2005).

Possible tendencies towards peace journalism appear in social variables and in the expectations for conflict resolution or transformation. The newspapers analyzed in this study show that people-oriented sources, lesser use of victimizing language and military discourse, and a win-win orientation can be promoted more easily than other dimensions as viable professional peace journalism practices. Like other components of conflict coverage, these findings might serve to steer efforts at promoting peace journalism.

Notes

1. The study was made possible thanks to a grant awarded by the Faculty Research Program of the Israel Association for Canadian Studies and Foreign Affairs Canada. The author is grateful for the friendly support given to the study by the Toda Institute for Global Peace and Policy Research, and by Toda's Peace Journalism group. The field team led by Keren Tamam, with the participation of Noa Koch and Gabriela Bar-On, and the cooperation with the Simon Fraser University research team, led by Bob Hackett and Birgitta Schroeder, made invaluable contributions to the study both in the fieldwork and in suggesting ideas and interpretations.
2. Kalb M., *The Israeli-Hezbollah War of 2006: The Media as a Weapon in Asymmetrical Conflict.* 2007. Faculty Research Working Papers Series R-29, John F. Kennedy School of Government - Harvard University, February, 8-11, http://ksgnotes1.harvard.edu/research/wpaper.nsf/rwp/RWP07-012.
    Reuters FACTBOX, http://www.reuters.com/article/latestCrisis/idUSL08118992; BBC Day-by-day: Lebanon crisis, http://news.bbc.co.uk/2/hi/middle_east/5179434.stm.
3. Harel, A. and A. Issascharoff. 2008. *34 Days: Israel, Hezbollah, and the War in Lebanon,* New York: Palgrave MacMillan, April; Al-Jazeera Timeline: Lebanon conflict, Aug. 17, 2006; Kalb, op. cit.
4. CBC News In Depth, August 14, 2006, http://www.cbc.ca/news/background/middleeast-crisis/index.html; BBC Day-by-day: Lebanon crisis op. cit.
5. Kalb, op. cit.
6. Koren-Dinar, R., "TGI Survey: 7% Less Exposure to the Daily Press," The Marker (Haaretz), January 30, 2007, 22.
7. http://www.torontosun.com.

References

Becker, J. 1982. "Communication and peace: The empirical and theoretical relation between two categories in social sciences." *Journal of Peace Research*, 19(3): 227-40.

Bläsi, B. 2004. "Peace Journalism and the News Production Process." *Conflict & Communication Online*, 3(1 & 2) www.cco.regener-online.de. See also *Conflict and Communication Online*, 4(2), 2005; 5(2), 2006; 6(1) 2007; 6 (2), 2007).

Dimitrova, D. V., and J. J. Stromback. 2005. *Framing of the Iraq War in the Elite Newspapers in Sweden and the United States,* paper presented at the ICA Journalism Studies Interest Group, New York.

Galtung, J. 1986. "On the role of the media in worldwide security and peace." In T. Varis (Ed.), *Peace and Communication* (pp. 249-66). San Jose, Costa Rica: Universidad para La Paz.

Galtung, J. 1998. *Peace journalism: What, why, who, how, when, where.* Paper presented in the workshop, "What are journalists for?" TRANSCEND, Taplow Court, UK, September 3–6.

Galtung, J. 2002. Media: Peace journalism. Retrieved September 25, 2003, from https://www.nicr.ca/programs/PeaceJournalism.htm.

Hackett, R. A. 2006. "Is peace journalism possible? Three frameworks for assessing structure and agency in news media." *Conflict and communication online,* 5(2).

Hackett, R. A., and R. Gruneau, 2000. *The Missing News: Filters and blind spots in Canada's Press.* Ottawa/Toronto: CCPA, Garamond.

Hanitzsch, T. 2004a. "Journalists as peacekeeping force? Peace journalism and mass communication theory." *Journalism Studies* 5 (4).

Hanitzsch, T. 2004b. "The peace journalism problem: Failure of news people—or failure on analysis?" in T. Hanitzsch et al. (eds.), *Public Communication and Conflict Resolution in an Asian Setting.* Jakarta: Friedrich Ebert Stiftung.

Höijer, B, S. Nohrstedt, and R. Ottosen. 2002. "The Kosovo War in the Media—Analysis of a Global discursive Order." *Conflict & Communication Online* No. 2 2002. www.cco.regener-online.de. See also http://www.immi.se/intercultural/nr10/.

Journalism and War Debate, Open Democracy, http://www.opendemocracy.net/debates/debate-8-92.jsp, particularly, 2003: February 20, *Witnessing the Truth* by David Loyn; February 26, *Witnessing Whose Truth?* By Des Freeman; May 15, The Threat of Better Journalism? By Danny Schechter, http://www.opendemocracy.net/debates/article-8-92-1227.jsp.

Kaid, L. L., Harville, B., Ballotti, J., and M. Wawrzyniak. 1993. Telling the Gulf War Story: Coverage in five papers. In B. S. Greenberg, and W. Glantz (eds.), *Desert Storm and the Mass Media.* Cresskill, NJ: Hampton Press.

Kempf, W. 1999. *Deescalation-oriented conflict coverage? The Northern Ireland and Israeli-Palestinian peace processes in the German press.* Diskussionsbeiträge der Projektgruppe Friedensforschung Konstanz, No. 45.

Kempf, W. 2001. "News media and conflict escalation - a comparative study of the Gulf War coverage in American and European media." In: S.A. Nohrstedt and R. Ottosen (eds.). *Journalism and the New World Order.* Vol. I. Gulf War, National News Discourses and Globalization. Göteborg: Nordicom.

Kempf, W. 2003. "Constructive conflict coverage—A social-psychological research and development program." *Conflict & Communication online,* 2 (2). www.cco.regener-online.de.

Kempf, W., M. Reimann and H. Luostarinen. 2000. "News media and conflict escalation: A comparative study of Gulf War coverage in the US and Europe media," in S. A. Nohrstedt & R. Ottosen, (eds.). *Journalism and the new world order: Gulf War, national news discourses, and globalization.* Göteborg: NORDICOM.

Knightley, P. 2000. "War journalism under fire." Committee for Peace in the Balkans. Access to http://www.peaceinbalkans.freeserve.co.uk.

Lynch, J. 2006. "What's so great about peace journalism?" *Conflict and Communication Online* 5 (2), www.cco.regener-online.de.

Lynch, J., and McGoldrick, A. 2005. *Peace Journalism.* Stroud, UK: Hawthorn Press.

McGoldrick, A., and J. Lynch. 1997, "The Peace Journalism Option." In *Transcend Website (Peace Journalism)* http://www.transcend.org.

McGoldrick, A., and J. Lynch. 2000. "Peace Journalism—How to Do It?" In *Transcend Website (Peace Journalism)* http://www.transcend.org.

McGoldrick, A., and J. Lynch. 2005. *Peace Journalism.* Stroud, Gloucestershire, UK: Hawthorn Press.

Ross, S.D. 2006. "(De-) Constructing conflict: A focused review of war and peace journalism." *Conflict and Communication Online* 5(2).

Sabine, W. 2005. "Covering the *war* in *Iraq:* Frame choice in American and German national newspapers." *Journal of Intercultural Communication,* Issue 10, December.

Shinar, D. 2003. "Peace Process in Cultural Conflict: The Role of the Media." *Conflict and Communication Online,* 2 (1), www.cco.regener-online.de.

Shinar, D. 2007. "Peace Journalism: The State of the Art." *Conflict & Communication online* 6 (1), www.cco.regener-online.de.

Ting Lee, S., and C. C. Maslog. 2005. "War or Peace Journalism? Asian Newspaper Coverage of Conflicts." *Journal of Communication*, June, pp. 311-329.

Does Anybody Practice Peace Journalism? A Cross-National Comparison of Press Coverage of the Afghanistan and Israeli-Hezbollah Wars[1]

Robert A. Hackett and Birgitta Schroeder
with NewsWatch Canada

Introduction

In various countries, and at the international level, advocacy groups and networks have arisen with the aim of democratizing the media, as a distinct institutional field (McChesney, 2004; Hackett and Carroll, 2006). One of the most interesting reform movements—peace journalism (PJ)—has emerged within the ranks of media professionals themselves. PJ's underlying assumptions arguably include the following:

1. News media are participants, not detached observers, in conflict situations; notwithstanding western journalism's "regime of objectivity," their presence unavoidably affects the course of conflicts (Lynch and McGoldrick, 2005a; Peleg, 2006).

2. Too often—whether through their subservience to state propaganda or other dominant political and economic forces, their over-accessing of extremists, journalistic routines of sourcing and objectivity, or other mechanisms (Hackett, 2007)—news media exacerbate conflict, contributing to its escalation at the expense of offering openings for peaceful options. Thus, conventional reporting of conflict too often amounts to "war journalism," which has the potential impact of creating perceptions and incentives, on the part of both policymakers and broader populations, that lead to conflict escalation. As Tehranian (2002) has put it, the "envy and hatred generated by global communication seems to have outpaced mutual understanding, respect, and tolerance."

3. Journalists have an "ethic of responsibility" to take into account the foreseeable consequences of their behavior, and to adjust their actions

31

accordingly. If reporting-as-usual constitutes war journalism, peace journalism calls on journalists to incorporate into their professional ethos a conscious choice in favor of peace, as an affirmation of their human responsibilities (Lynch and McGoldrick, 2005a; Ross, 2006; Spencer, 2005).

As a "point for contestation" and "a campaign for change capable of uniting reform-minded journalists and activists across different media and different countries," (Lynch and McGoldrick, 2005b), peace journalism draws on the insights of the emergent disciplines of conflict analysis and peace studies pioneered by Johan Galtung. It calls on journalism to look beyond the overt violence of war and to attend to the "ABC" context of conflict: Attitudes, Behavior, and Contradictions, including underlying patterns of structural and cultural violence. Journalists, in this view, should identify a range of stakeholders broader than the "two sides" directly engaged in confrontation and reframe conflict as a "cat's cradle" of relationships between the various stakeholders rather than as a tug-of-war between two parties in which one side's gain is the other's loss. Peace journalism also calls on journalists to distinguish stated demands from underlying needs and objectives, to access voices working for creative and non-violent solutions, and to keep eyes open for ways of transforming and transcending the hardened lines of conflict. In that process, journalists would need to expand their range of sources beyond the political and official elites who typically comprise the primary definers of media agendas, and avoid both victimizing, demonizing or emotive language and dichotomous framing. The hope, the expectation, is that through such practices, journalists can both offer more complete and accurate accounts of conflicts and help create an environment more conducive to resolving or transforming conflicts away from war.

As developed by internationally acclaimed practitioners and educators like Lynch and McGoldrick (2005a), PJ's main impetus has been to improve journalism. However, PJ also potentially offers an analytical lens for scholarly research on media representations of war. That literature, of course, is considerable. In a "critical" vein, many textual analyses demonstrate that war news has "generally been characterized by an identification with one or the home side of the conflict, military triumphantist language, an action-oriented focus, and a superficial narrative with little context, background or historical perspective" (Knightley, 2000, cited in Maslog et al., 2006). The literature on the 1991 Gulf War and the 2003 U.S.-led invasion of Iraq is particularly rich, much of it focusing on inaccuracies and the receptivity of media to state-promulgated pro-war propaganda (e.g., Bennett and Paletz, 1994; Mowlana, Gerbner and Schiller, 1992; Kellner, 1992; Spencer, 2005; Allan and Zelizer, 2004, part 3). By contrast, another strand of literature—more "conservative" in that it implies the need to link media more closely to the forces of social order—focuses on media as a tool for insurgent terrorists (e.g., Klopfenstein, 2006; Liebes and Kampf, 2004). Other studies attempt to show bias for one or another combatant and their perspectives, in particular vis-à-vis the Israeli-Palestinian conflict, one that has so much cultural and political resonance elsewhere in the world (e.g., Muravchik, 2003; Philo and Berry, 2004). Relatively few studies examine the role of media in putative peace processes (e.g., Wolfsfeld, 2004).[2]

The conflict analysis/PJ approach shifts the prism. It certainly does not dismiss the questions of bias for/against one side, or journalism's relationship to the state, as irrelevant; far from it. Rather, PJ highlights these issues in the context of how media representations may contribute to the escalation or de-escalation of conflict. Until quite recently though, few studies had used PJ to summarize and evaluate media coverage.[3] Two pioneering studies deserve mention. Lynch (2006) analyzed British newspaper articles on the "Iran nuclear crisis" in 2005, counting the frequency of five key propositions, inspired by conflict analysis, about the conflict's scope and potential solutions. He found that only a small proportion of articles presented the crisis across a broad field of conflict formation (notably, the Non-Proliferation Treaty), with various "exits" open in time and space. Instead, the coverage focused on Iran, the immediate conflict arena, in the present and near future. Methodologically, Lynch's approach has the advantage of quantitative precision, enabling comparisons between different newspapers. On the other hand, the approach is vulnerable to critiques of selectivity: how do we choose what specific propositions or themes would best enable journalism to contribute to conflict de-escalation? Moreover, if such propositions are unique to each conflict, the potential for comparative news analysis across conflicts is limited.

Maslog, Lee and Kim (2006) adopted a somewhat different approach. They devised a set of thirteen indicators to differentiate between war journalism and peace journalism in news coverage. Using these criteria to construct two respective scales, their study found a slight preponderance of PJ over war journalism in press coverage of the 2003 Iraq war in five Asian countries. Non-Muslim countries' newspapers, however, had a stronger war journalism framing and were more supportive of the U.S.-U.K. governments, compared to Muslim nations (Maslog, Lee and Kim, 2006). Such a result implies that country and religion, rather than the conscious practice of PJ, were significantly influential factors; quite different results might be obtained with respect to other conflicts with different protagonists.

The study by Maslog et al. provides a starting point for the current study in several respects. On the one hand, it provides a methodology that enables researchers to distinguish between, and assess the relative prominence of, different aspects of PJ in news content. The method also potentially enables a comparison of news coverage of different conflicts, using the PJ and war journalism scales. On the other hand, the study suggests a need for further exploration of the relationship between de-escalating aspects of news coverage, on the one hand, and, on the other hand, other aspects of news discourse, and external environments and influences on news content.

Critics have argued that PJ advocacy and scholarship have failed to sufficiently take into account the actual determinants, constraints and dynamics of news production, and thus may not be useful as a guide for working journalists (Hanitzsch, 2004). Lynch and McGoldrick (2005a) helpfully outline some of the "currents of analysis" in media theory that inform PJ, in a chapter entitled "Why is news the way it is?" but they do not develop the implications for identifying the obstacles and resources affecting the successful implementation of PJ. Conceptually, Hackett (2006, 2007) has begun that project, assessing the prospects of PJ in relation to the Herman/Chomsky "propaganda model" of the media, Pierre Bourdieu's field theory, and particularly, the Hierarchy of Influences model of Shoemaker and Reese (1996), which identifies five layers of influences on mass media content.[4] Such assessments clearly need to be informed by the practical experiences of journalists, peace activists, and others who seek to use communications media in conflict transformation and peace-building processes. But content analysis of existing news coverage can also play a role in identifying openings for peace-promoting communication.

Accordingly, as a contribution to PJ scholarship, the current study has a threefold purpose:

- First, it is a pedagogical exercise in media literacy. The research was conducted, and to some extent designed, by three teams of students in the NewsWatch Canada seminar at Simon Fraser University, under Hackett's supervision. It afforded an opportunity for future researchers to learn to read news critically through a PJ lens. The trade-off, of course, is that the sample bears the idiosyncracies of combining three separate studies, and the findings must be regarded as exploratory.

- Second, the researchers adapted and applied Maslog et al's variables and scales to the analysis of conflicts other than the Iraq war in hopes of furthering the development of a methodology useful for comparative analysis.
- Third, the study intended to help build an empirical base of data informed by a PJ perspective. It examines coverage by print- and web-based news outlets in four countries (Canada, the U.S., Israel, and Qatar), with respect to two different conflicts that occurred in summer 2006: the war, occurring mainly on Lebanese soil, between Israel and the Islamicist group Hezbollah; and the ongoing conflict in Afghanistan between NATO forces (including Canada and the U.S.) and the Taliban. The overriding objective was to identify news contexts in which the characteristics of PJ were most evident, with a view to speculating about changes in the ethos or structure of journalism that might constitute an enabling environment for the practices of PJ.

The specific research questions are these:

1. a.) What is the dominant frame—war or peace journalism—in the coverage of the Afghanistan and Lebanon conflicts in the press of the four countries? And
    b.) What characteristics of WJ and PJ are most salient?
2. Does the country of publication, and the involvement or non-involvement of that country in each of the two conflicts, affect the war/peace frame?
3. Is the war/peace frame influenced by, or correlated with, other aspects of the "news net" (Tuchman, 1978) and the news production/presentation process, viz., the political and market orientation of each newspaper, the organizational provenance of articles (news agencies vs. local staff), the locale of the story, the genre of article ("hard" news reports vs. others) and the types of sources accessed?

Methodology

This media content analysis is comprised of 522 articles published in summer 2006, from eight English-language Canadian, American and Israeli daily newspapers, and articles from four news outlets' websites (two Canadian, one Israeli, and one from Qatar). The three student research teams compiled the samples and coded their respective data sets.

The three samples were amalgamated and constitute the data sample for this study.

All collected articles discuss either the Afghan conflict or the Hezbollah/Israel conflict. Both the timing and original causes of these conflicts are much contested. Here, we simply highlight the events most relevant to our monitoring period. The Afghan conflict has been ongoing since the beginning of October 2001, when U.S. and U.K. forces attacked and invaded the country for the stated purpose of overthrowing the Taliban regime and capturing Osama bin Laden and his al Qaida associates, the alleged perpetrators of the September 11, 2001, terror attacks on U.S. soil. Canada has been part of the active NATO alliance (later expanded, and endorsed by the U.N.) from the beginning, and in February, 2006, renewed its commitment. This entailed an increase and re-deployment of its forces to the dangerous southern region, where Canadians engaged in fierce fighting against the Taliban. During the media monitoring period, 21 Canadian and 25 American troops died, along with many Taliban fighters and Afghan civilians.[5]

The Hezbollah-Israel conflict started on July 12, 2006, when the Israeli Defense Force (IDF) launched a series of air strikes and artillery fire on Lebanon (as well as naval blockades) in response to the Hezbollah's capture of two Israeli soldiers earlier that month (Hezbollah was hoping to provoke a prisoner exchange, as had occurred after prior similar incidents). Hezbollah responded with rockets aimed at northern Israel. Subsequent invasion by the IDF into southern Lebanon escalated into a full-blown war between Hezbollah and Israel, which lasted five weeks, until August 14, 2006, when an U.N.-mediated ceasefire came into effect. Both sides claimed victory. Lebanon, in particular southern Lebanon, saw most of its infrastructure demolished and the displacement of 915,762 civilians. Approximately 500,000 northern Israelis were displaced. The war took more than 1,200 Lebanese and 157 Israeli lives.[6] At the end of August, 2006, U.N. peacekeepers started deployment along the southern Lebanese border and the task of disarming Hezbollah. In September, 2006, Lebanese troops were stationed along the Israeli border for the first time in decades.

Sampling Methods

Group I looked at articles discussing the two conflicts published in the print press between July 1 and September 1, 2006. During the same time frame, Group II sampled articles on the Hezbollah-Israel conflict only.[7] Group III looked at articles posted on four news-outlets' websites and one newspaper between September 15 and September 29, 2006. Thus, Groups I and II analyzed articles covering the Hezbollah-Israel conflict throughout its duration, and Group III looked at articles covering the aftermath of the Hezbollah-Israel conflict.[8] The Afghan conflict has been ongoing, and articles reporting on the Afghan conflict throughout the above time periods were collected.[9] With the exception of Qatar, all publications and online news outlets represent countries that are directly involved in one of the two conflicts.

The sample universe included news, opinion/editorial, columns, interviews, features, and "focus" pieces. Letters to the editor, business, sports or other specialty sections were excluded. The sample also excluded the many articles making glancing references to one of the conflicts.[10]

Criteria for selecting the newspaper sample included publication in English, as well as the potential for the following comparisons: Israeli and Canadian papers (a funding requirement), conservative and left-liberal papers, "popular" tabloids and "quality" dailies, online and print publications, Western and Arab-based publications, and newspapers whose "home" country was directly involved in the conflict reported versus newspapers in non-combatant countries. These were ambitious criteria for a relatively small sample, and the results must be interpreted with considerable caution. The following news outlets were included (for the time-frame July 1 to September 1, 2006):

- Canadian newspapers: the *Globe and Mail*, the *National Post*, the *Toronto Star*, and the *Toronto Sun*.
- Israeli newspaper: the *Jerusalem Post* (English version only).
- American newspapers: the *New York Times* and the *New York Post*.

The following news outlets were utilized for the time period September 15 to 29, 2006.

- Canadian newspapers' websites: the *Globe and Mail* and the *National Post*.
- Israeli online news site: *Ha'aretz* (English version only).
- Israeli print press: the *Jerusalem Post*[11] (English version only).
- Arabian online news outlet: *al-Jazeera*[12] (English version only).

To maintain a workable sample size and an unbiased sample from all publications researched within the July 1 to September 1 timeframe, Group I and II employed the *constructed week* sampling method.[13] Group

III limited the timeframe for its online article sample to a two-week period, September 15 to 29, 2006. Online news outlets were chosen because of the growing importance of the Internet as a news source and to explore whether its technical capacities were being used to provide greater context and more diverse frames.

Organizational Variables and Conceptual Themes

The three groups used a collectively established codebook and variables. The basic unit of analysis was the individual article. Given that a thoroughly tested standard instrument measuring characteristics of peace journalism is not yet available, the team developed its own, creating a coding sheet with 76 variables loosely based on Maslog et al. (2006).

Besides "identification" variables such as case number and coder, fourteen variables of an organizational nature captured the publication date, publication, article genre, headline, story locale, the conflict discussed, etc. Thirty-three variables identified "sources and actors" (individuals, groups, institutions). Only the "highest" form of access was coded for each category of source/actor, on a four-point scale: first source quoted or paraphrased; quoted later in the article; mentioned but not quoted or paraphrased; and not mentioned at all.

Indicators for peace journalism or war journalism were based on Galtung's characteristics of the two genres (as elaborated in Maslog et al., 2006). The indicators were operationalized into twenty-six variables. Ten of these variables were used as indicators of war journalism:

1. Does the story discuss the *visible effects* of war?
2. Is the story *elite-oriented*?
3. Is the story *differences-oriented*?
4. Does the story discuss the *here and now*?
5. Does the story report on *direct violence*?
6. Does the story *dichotomize the good and bad*?
7. Is the story *two-party oriented*?
8. Is the story *zero-sum oriented*?[14]
9. Does the article discuss *military options*?
10. Is the article overall *supportive of "our" role*?[15]

Ten parallel "counterpart" variables constituted peace journalism indicators:

1. Does the story report on the *invisible effects of war*?[16]
2. Is the story *people-oriented*?[17]

3. Is the story *agreement-oriented*?
4. Does the story discuss the *long-term causes* and/or *consequences of war*?
5. Does it report on *structural and/or cultural violence*?[18]
6. Does the story *avoid good versus bad framing*?
7. Is the story *multi-party oriented*?
8. Does the story report *win-win or lose-lose options*?[19]
9. Does it discuss *peaceful options*?
10. Is the article *critical of our role*?

Each of these twenty variables was coded "yes"/"no," enabling us to produce a score of 0 to 10 for each article with regard to WJ and PJ respectively. With one exception (question # 6), the paired questions were not mutually exclusive—it was possible to answer both questions the same way ("yes," or "no"). These scales were our main dependent variables in the subsequent analysis.

All three groups conducted four intra-group inter-coder reliability tests (percent agreement).[20] The last set of inter-coder reliability tests resulted in the following average agreement: Group I - 81.7%; Group II - 79.0%; Group III - 85.0%.

Combined Sample

The three data sets from the three groups were amalgamated into one, resulting in 624 articles. All articles were scrutinized for coding inconsistencies, corrected or eliminated as necessary. The final data set consists of 522 articles. To facilitate analysis, several variables were re-coded, notably the "sources and actors." This process also created several new variables, notably, the WJ and PJ scale,[21] and the aggregated source types described in Table 6.

Findings

Frequency of War and Peace Journalism Characteristics

To what extent are the characteristics of war journalism and peace journalism prevalent in coverage of the two conflicts? By aggregating the samples from the several countries and conflicts, Table 1 highlights a sharp contrast in terms of the relative frequency of each of the characteristics in our war and peace journalism scales. On average, each WJ factor appears in 51.9 percent of the articles, whereas each PJ factor is present in only 31.6 percent. Put differently, the average WJ score for each article is 5.19 out of 10, while the average PJ score is just 3.16.

The high WJ score is particularly accounted for by the news focus on immediate events, elites, the visible effects of war, and direct (rather than structural or cultural) violence.

By contrast, the most salient characteristic of PJ is a "negative" one, an absence rather than a presence: in 55.2 percent of articles, the conflict is *not* clearly represented as a dyadic struggle between good and evil. This finding is subject to different interpretations. Conventions of objectivity may have contributed to stylistically neutral coverage, or alternatively, pro-Israeli sympathies in the Western press may have been offset by the fact that Israel was the party unleashing the greatest level of violence (the bombing of Lebanon).

The second most frequent PJ characteristic (53.6 percent of articles) is the framing of the conflicts as involving multiple parties rather than simply two sides. Perhaps the complex nature of these two conflicts virtually forced journalists to attend to the plurality of stakeholders, including civilians trapped in the middle, and intervening governments and inter-governmental agencies from outside the region.

The correlation of WJ/PJ scores with the distribution of topics during the coverage is not coincidental, as the two variables are not entirely conceptually independent: war journalism is constituted, in part, by how the topical focus of "the story" is defined. But neither are they completely dependent; even in reports about direct violence, it is possible to "do" PJ. For most topics, WJ criteria are more frequent than PJ. The few topics where this does not occur are: civilian destruction; other current impacts of war; peace discussions; human interest; peace protests; and reconstruction. But these topics are not the most frequent, especially compared to elite diplomacy, political debate (also usually dominated by elites), battles, and other military moves.

We now turn attention to the relationship between WJ and PJ scores and other variables in the news production and presentation process—respectively, the country and newspaper of publication, the organizational provenance of articles (e.g., wire services or regular staff), the geographical focus of each news story, the genre of article, and the accessing of sources.

Nationality of Publication

Table 2 (below) shows the comparative number of stories about the two conflicts in the press of each of the four countries, as well as the WJ and PJ mean for each category of articles. The results are consistent with national "bias" in the press of the four nations. Only Canada, the

Table 1
Indicators of War Journalism and Peace Journalism

War Journalism Approach	N	% of Mentions (N = 522)	% of Sampled Articles
Visible effects of war	300	11.07	57.5
Elite-oriented	340	12.55	65.1
Differences-oriented	231	8.53	44.3
Focus on here and now	401	14.80	76.8
Reports on direct violence	296	10.93	56.7
Dichotomizes the good & bad	234	8.64	44.8
Two-party oriented	179	6.61	34.3
Zero-sum oriented	226	8.34	43.3
Discusses military options	235	8.67	45.0
Supports "our" role	267	9.86	51.1
TOTAL	2709	100.00	
AVERAGE			51.9
Peace Journalism Approach			
Invisible effects of war	238	14.42	45.6
People-oriented	165	9.99	31.6
Agreement-oriented	90	5.45	17.2
Causes or consequences of war	138	8.36	26.4
Structural or cultural violence	139	8.42	26.6
Avoids good/bad dichotomy	288	17.44	55.2
Multi-party oriented	280	16.96	53.6
Win-win or lose-lose oriented	90	5.45	17.2
Discusses peaceful options	118	7.15	22.6
Critical of "our" role	105	6.36	20.1
TOTAL	1651	100.00	
AVERAGE			31.6

Table 2
Country of Publication by Conflict by War & Peace Journalism Mean Score

Country	Conflict Focus	N	War J Mean	Peace J Mean
Canada	Afghanistan	101	6.02	2.36
Canada	Hezbollah	61	5.15	3.77
USA	Afghanistan	7	4.43	2.71
USA	Hezbollah	44	5.66	3.34
Israel	Afghanistan	1	9.00	6.00
Israel	Hezbollah	75	5.32	4.04
Qatar	Afghanistan	11	6.27	2.18
Qatar	Hezbollah	15	5.67	3.07
	TOTAL N	315		

WJ * Source Country & Afghan Conflict: $F = 1.482$, $df = 11$, $p = 0.137 > 0.05$
PJ * Source Country & Afghan Conflict: $F = 3.788$, $df = 11$, $p = 0.000 < 0.05$
WJ * Source Country & Hezbollah Conflict: $F = 7.451$, $df = 10$, $p = 0.263 > 0.05$
PJ * Source Country & Hezbollah Conflict: $F = 19.293$, $df = 10$, $p = 0.000 < 0.05$
Note: a new file with reduced data, n=315, was created. All articles from Group II were taken out for this table, due to sampling inconsistency re Afghan conflict

country most heavily involved, gave Afghanistan more coverage than Israel/Hezbollah. Canadian press coverage of the Afghanistan conflict was more "belligerent" (on the WJ and PJ scales) than its coverage of Lebanon, where no Canadian troops were deployed (but where Canadian citizens, mostly of Arabic heritage, were killed).

By contrast, in our sample of Israeli and U.S. press coverage, Afghanistan is almost "the forgotten war" (Ricchiardi, 2006). Given the conflict on its own borders and the occasional rockets targeting its cities, that is understandable in the Israeli case. But the Afghan war barely shows on U.S. press radar screens, notwithstanding the presence of U.S. troops and the remnants of the al-Qaeda and Taliban forces that allegedly launched the 9/11 terror attacks in 2001. One can surmise that America's vastly greater and costlier presence in Iraq is far more newsworthy; and the dramatic nature of the Hezbollah conflict, and exceptionally strong historical, political, and cultural sympathy for Israel in the United States, virtually makes Israel a "home team" in U.S. reporting of the Middle East.

Al-Jazeera (Qatar) divided its attention fairly evenly between the two conflicts. Qatar is directly involved in neither conflict; however, both are of interest to al-Jazeera's Arabic audience and sponsors.

Newspaper Type

What about differences within the press of each country? Does the type of newspaper matter? Are so-called "quality" dailies, oriented towards intellectual, economic and political elites, less simplistic and thus less prone to conflict-exacerbating stereotypes when compared to down-market tabloid papers that reputedly trade in moral outrage and Manichean narratives? Are dailies with a "right-wing" political reputation more warlike than their left-liberal counterparts? Are online editions of papers, with their much greater technical capacity for elaboration and for accessing a wider range of voices, more conducive to PJ?

Table 3 does not clearly confirm these assumptions. Table 3 ranks the twelve news outlets from most "warlike" to least, based on the overall difference between the average WJ and PJ scores of their articles. With respect to the political dimension, on the one hand, in Canada, the reputedly right-wing *National Post* is more warlike than the centrist *Globe & Mail*, which in turn is somewhat more warlike than the left-liberal

Table 3
Newspaper by War and Peace Journalism Mean Score

Newspaper	N	War J Mean	Peace J Mean	Between-Mean Difference
Globe & Mail online	66	6.47	2.35	4.12
New York Post	10	5.20	1.50	3.70
National Post online	29	5.79	2.41	3.38
al-Jazeera	25	6.04	2.72	3.32
National Post	33	5.03	3.00	2.03
New York Times	42	5.62	3.60	2.02
Toronto Sun	23	4.04	2.26	1.78
Jerusalem Post (Fall)	54	5.65	3.89	1.76
Jerusalem Post (Summer)	127	4.54	3.05	1.49
Globe & Mail	49	5.27	4.10	1.17
Toronto Star	39	4.10	3.31	0.79
Ha'aretz	25	4.64	4.56	0.08
TOTAL/AVERAGE	522	5.19	3.16	2.03

WJ * Newspaper: $F = 4.832$, $df = 11$, $p = 0.00 < 0.05$
PJ * Newspaper: $F = 5.295$, $df = 11$, $p = 0.00 < 0.05$

Toronto Star—as a political interpretation would predict. In Israel, the conservative *Jerusalem Post* is indeed more warlike than the decidedly more liberal *Ha'aretz*. On the other hand, the *Globe & Mail*'s online edition is more hawkish than the *National Post*'s. It is worth bearing in mind that in a study of the British press treatment of the Iranian nuclear crisis, Lynch (2006) found that the left-wing *Guardian* ranked below more conservative dailies in peace journalism attributes.

With respect to types of newspapers, the two tabloid papers (*New York Post* and *Toronto Sun*) are on balance more hawkish than their broadsheet counterparts; although more precisely, the broadsheet papers, with their longer articles and their more civic and "literate" news values, rank higher on both the WJ and PJ scales, compared to tabloids. It is reasonable to assume that the length of an article correlates positively with higher scores on both scales. (Also note the small size of the tabloid sample, however.)

It is the online editions, however, that offer the greatest surprise. They are the most hawkish of the three types, notwithstanding their potential to offer the kind of elaborated and diverse explanations of conflict that PJ calls for. This may be because the online editions, driven by competitive pressures to attract net users' attention, publish and highlight their most dramatic stories on their websites, rather than long opinion or background features. Alternatively, the limitations of online search engines and of archives provided, may have skewed the findings, e.g., there may be supplementary material on the websites that are not archived. And again, the sample size must be considered.

Organizational Provenance

Do articles provided by national or transnational news services, such as Associated Press or Reuters, differ in their WJ/PJ content when compared to material written by a news outlet's own staff? Maslog et al. (2006) found that such was the pattern, in the particular case of five Asian nations' press coverage of the 2003 Iraq war. Critics might object that this discrepancy was specific to Maslog's particular case, reflecting the pro-Western orientation of the dominant news agencies, and the more critical stance towards the Iraq war on the part of Asian governments and publics, particularly Muslim ones. But our own research yields a similar result. Reports from newspapers' own staff ranked lowest (4.98, N = 324) out of ten coded organizational sources of articles on the WJ scale. Ranking above it are Reuters (5.00), Canadian Press (5.15), Associated Press (5.86), Agence France Presse (6.33, but N = 3 only), other news agencies (6.33), with mixed, unknown or other sources in the middle of the rankings. Conversely, on the PJ scale, newspapers' own staff ranked third highest (3.17) out of ten organizational types, surpassed only by other newspapers (4.00, but N = 4 only), and other sources (4.70). The news agencies all had lower PJ scores: Reuters (3.08), AP (2.57), Canadian Press (2.23), AFP (0.67), and other news agencies (2.67). Interestingly, Reuters is less hawkish than the other agencies on both scales, perhaps a tribute to its carefully nurtured reputation for nation-transcending objectivity.

Noting that the research literature supports the local/news agency disparity in war/peace journalism frames, Maslog et al. (2006) speculate that "Western news agencies tend to emphasize war/conflict/violence" and describe developing nations as "the scenes of disasters or great violence," probably because the agencies "are reporting mainly for their local Western audiences who have been raised on a diet of conflict and violence in the news." Our own previous research, along with much else, supports the notion that news of the global south reported in Canadian media, at least, comprises "coups, earthquakes and hostages" (Hackett, 1989). One could go further though to speculate that foreign wire copy is typically used in newsrooms to "describe and convey daily situation updates of the war" (Maslog et al., 2006) rather than to provide human interest and background feature pieces, which provide greater scope for PJ practices but arguably do not travel as well across cultures. Conversely, local papers are better equipped, and face higher demand, to produce human-interest stories with local angles—more fertile ground for PJ.

Story Locale

The research team categorized each article into one of ten geographical regions or locales, the geographical setting of the story. (Often this coincided with the dateline indicating the point from which the report was filed, but not always.)

Table 4 ranks the articles from the ten regions according to their WJ and PJ averages. Arguably, those locales scoring highest in WJ tend to be either war zones or the capitals of countries involved directly in war. Lower WJ scores are found in Europe, the rest of the world (including the Middle East apart from Israel, Palestine, and Lebanon)—areas where there was significant support, in the case of the Lebanon conflict, for an early ceasefire, and where relevant newsworthy stories were not about battles, but about diplomatic efforts or peace protests. Interestingly, within the U.S. and Canada, stories from the capital cities, as centers of

Table 4
Story Locale by War Journalism/Peace Journalism Mean Scores

Locale	Rank	War Journalism Mean	Rank	Peace Journalism Mean	N
Afghanistan	1	5.95	10	2.48	65
Washington DC	2	5.79	8	2.68	19
Ottawa	3	5.52	9	2.66	29
Lebanon	4	5.39	4	3.27	140
Canada (other than Ottawa)	5	5.14	6	2.90	29
Israel & Palestine	6	5.12	5	3.23	151
USA (other than Washington DC)	7	4.38	2	4.00	21
Middle East (other than Lebanon, Israel or Palestine)	8	4.24	1	4.81	21
Europe	9	4.10	3	3.62	21
Elsewhere (other than locales listed here)	10	4.00	7	2.74	23
OVERALL AVERAGE/ TOTAL		5.19		3.19	519

WJ * 1st Story Locale: $F = 2.330$, $df = 13$, $p = 0.005 < 0.05$
PJ * 1st Story Locale: $F = 2.338$, $df = 13$, $p = 0.005 < 0.05$

official discourse, had higher WJ and lower PJ scores than stories from elsewhere in those two countries.

Article Genre

In the Western press, and particularly in North America, the professional practices of "objectivity" and "facticity" (Tuchman, 1978) are embedded, in part, through the separation of apparently factual news reports from the expression of writers' personal opinions or the analysis of the context of news events. Do the latter genres lend themselves more readily to the kind of elaboration called for by PJ?

Our data are suggestive but hardly definitive. By contrast with opinion articles and background features, news reports are relatively low in both scales. On PJ, they averaged 2.98, compared to 4.36 for opinion pieces, 3.75 for features, 3.18 for editorials, and an overall mean of 3.16. On WJ, news reports averaged 5.17, compared to 5.56 for features, 5.39 for editorials, 5.36 for opinion pieces, and an overall mean of 5.19. These results may reflect an unavoidable ambiguity in the two scales: all other things being equal, shorter items are likely to score lower on both scales than longer ones, and news reports tend to be shorter than features. Moreover, news reports comprise such a high proportion of the sample (407 of 522 coded items) that they largely determine the norm and make comparison across genres less statistically meaningful. Nevertheless, we can surmise that the generally higher scores for opinion/editorial and feature articles indicate that their greater potential for discursive elaboration was deployed both "for" and "against" the peaceful resolution of conflict.

Sources

The clearest finding to emerge from our study is the dramatic relationship between war/peace framing and the use of sources in journalistic accounts. As the critiques by peace journalism theorists predict (Lynch and McGoldrick, 2005a), conventional news coverage of war embodies a hierarchy of access that privileges military officers, government officials and politicians over civilians, publics, civil society organizations, and peace activists.

Table 5 indicates that this hierarchy of access roughly correlates with the war/peace framing of articles. It displays, in descending order, the average WJ and PJ scores for articles in which each type of source is quoted (whether initially or later in the article). By using this table to calculate the difference for each source-type from the overall PJ and WJ means, it is possible to divide the source-types into three groups.

Those groups with above average WJ and below average PJ scores are (in descending order of the sum of their differences from the WJ and PJ means) NATO, military officials, Afghan President Karzai, Canadian Prime Minister Harper, U.S. President Bush (all three being leaders of countries at war in Afghanistan), pro-government politicians, and government officials.

Those groups with the greatest combined "surfeit" above the average PJ score and "deficit" below the average WJ scale are (in descending order) peace activists, "other" international governmental organizations, Lebanon's Prime Minister Siniora, humanitarian groups and NGOs, the European Union, generic references to any country as a source (e.g., "Syria said today…"), "other" sources, civilians and refugees, and independent experts. Politically, these groups can be described as those whose political and professional work is consistent with peaceful conflict-resolution, state or inter-state institutions that tended to favor an early cease-fire in Lebanon, the victims of war (civilians, Lebanon's leader), and civil society (non-state) experts.

The remaining sources could be described as "mixed", either above average, or below average, on both WJ and PJ scales. The most interesting are the following:

- Rank-and-file soldiers were notably less "militarist" than senior military spokespeople.
- Domestic and foreign publics (civil society interest groups, public opinion) were arguably ambivalent. A "support the troops" emotional response may offset the reluctance of public opinion in many countries to favor war as an option.
- Articles quoting Israeli Prime Minister Olmert were more "dovish" than those quoting other wartime leaders, although his country was centrally involved in a war. This probably reflects in large part his comparatively more frequent appearance in the newspaper with the highest PJ score, *Ha'aretz*; but, more indirectly, it may indicate a greater degree of political diversity in the Israeli press, compared to Canada and the U.S.

Notwithstanding the ambiguities inherent in the several "mixed" cases noted above, Table 6 graphically demonstrates the strong correlation between source access, and war/peace framing. For this table, we combined most of the several dozen source-types into five main categories: military, political elite, independent experts/observers, anti-western insurgents, and civilians. For each category, we recorded only the "highest" degree of access (first quoted, later quoted, or not quoted) in each article. Consider the WJ and PJ scores of articles in which each category of source is the first or "lead" source; it is easy to compute the amount by which the WJ mean surpasses the PJ mean. In descending order, they are the military (the average WJ score exceeds the PJ score by 4.08); anti-Western insurgents (2.92); political elites of various stripes (2.16); independent experts (0.70); and civilians (0.42). Moreover, in seven out of ten cases, there are ascending or descending linear relationships between the three degrees of access, and the WJ or PJ score. For instance, the higher the degree of access accorded to the military, the higher the WJ score, and the lower the PJ score. (In a three-point access scale, such linear relationships would occur randomly only one-third of the time.)

Conclusion

The results of this study must be regarded as very preliminary for two reasons. First, it is based on a sample that is limited in scale and

Table 5

Sources by War & Peace Journalism Mean Score

Rank	Actor	WJ Mean	N	Actor	PJ Mean	N
1	Taliban	8.00	5	Peace activists	5.57	7
2	Captive soldier	7.00	1	al-Qaida	5.00	1
3	Military officer, spkmn	6.44	157	Other internatl gov't org.	4.88	8
4	Other anti-Western grps	6.40	5	PM Siniora (Lebanon)	4.50	10
5	NATO	6.28	18	Government/country	4.48	42
6	PM Harper (Canada)	6.20	35	Humanitarian grps, NGO	4.39	28
7	PM Olmert (Israel)	6.20	51	Domestic public	4.12	26
8	Pres. Karzai (Afghan.)	6.15	20	Other head of gov't	4.10	63
9	Domestic public	5.96	26	U.N. peacekeepers	4.00	18
10	Non-domestic public	5.83	12	Non-domestic public	4.00	12
11	Hezbollah	5.61	49	Captive Israeli soldier	4.00	1
12	U.N. peacekeepers	5.61	18	Other	3.81	43
13	Media	5.54	63	Other anti-Western grps	3.80	5
14	Opposition politician	5.48	52	Civilians	3.73	69
15	Soldiers (not sr. military)	5.45	20	U.N.	3.68	71
16	Gov't politician	5.43	117	Opposition politician	3.46	52
17	Gov't officials	5.38	155	Hezbollah	3.45	49
18	Other head of gov't	5.30	63	Independent experts	3.43	61
19	Pres. Bush	5.28	29	European Union	3.40	5
20	U.N.	5.20	71	Taliban	3.40	5
21	Soldiers' families	5.04	28	Media	3.30	63
22	al-Qaida	5.00	1	PM Olmert (Israel)	3.29	51
23	Government/country	4.95	42	Soldiers (not sr. mil.)	3.20	20
24	Civilians	4.67	69	Government officials	3.05	155
25	Other	4.58	43	Government politician	3.04	117
26	Independent experts	4.57	61	Soldiers' families	2.82	28
27	PM Siniora (Lebanon)	4.20	10	PM Harper (Canada)	2.77	35
28	Humanitarian grps, NGO	4.18	28	Pres. Bush	2.72	29
29	European Union	3.80	5	Pres. Karzai (Afghan.)	2.60	20
30	PM Blair (U.K.)	3.75	12	Military officer, spkmn	2.49	157
31	Peace activists	3.71	7	PM Blair (U.K.)	2.17	12
32	Other internatl gov't org.	3.25	8	NATO	2.00	18
	TOTAL/AVERAGE	5.19	1281		3.16	1281

timeframe. Second, the empirical indicators of peace journalism need to be refined; they are derived from a literature that was initially intended as a guide to journalism practice rather than to empirical research. Nevertheless, the results of this study are broadly consistent with previous research, and they are suggestive. They demonstrate that the characteristics of war and peace journalism broadly correlate with other aspects of news production and presentation.

War journalism was associated with the topical focus on military actions and elite talk and with the news outlet's home country's involvement in war. This focus is consistent with such well-recognized news values as confrontation, drama, negativity, elite orientation, and national interest.

War journalism was also associated more with international news agencies than local staff copy and with the capital cities of countries at war. In our analysis, we inferred the influence of factors that are already recognized in the sociology of news production and of political discourse. Above all, war journalism correlates with the high degree of access accorded to military and government sources, which are privileged over voices of civil society. All of these factors operate in peacetime journalism but arguably are intensified in wartime.

Conversely, higher PJ scores, where they occurred, were associated with the multilateral nature of the conflicts (rendering their Manichean dichotomization more difficult), with some of the op/ed articles, with local staff writers rather than agency copy, with locales removed from war zones and the belligerents' capitals, and with access (when it was granted, presumably on grounds of perceived newsworthiness) accorded to peace activists, victims of war, and independent experts.

Parenthetically, in our sample, Israeli newspapers appear to be somewhat less "warlike" than their North American counterparts. Why is this the case? It may reflect the wider ideological range in Israel of both the political party system and of Israel's press, where traditions of partisanship contrast with North American journalism's "regime of objectivity" (Hackett and Zhao, 1998). For both reasons, there may be more space in Israel's political culture for vigorous criticism of the home government, even in wartime. Or perhaps Israel's longer experience on the edge of war has created a stronger urgency, in some quarters, for the need to pursue peaceful options. Alternatively, the finding may indicate a limitation in the measurement or even the concept of peace journalism. It may be possible to obtain a relatively high score on the PJ scale through providing context and evincing a "liberal" sympathy for suffering on all sides

Table 6
Source-Type by War & Peace Journalism Mean Score

Type	Lead Quote	Later Quoted	Not Quoted
Military	(N = 89)	(N = 81)	(N = 352)
War J Mean	6.45	6.09	4.67
Peace J Mean	2.37	2.83	3.44

WJ * Military: F = 28.007, df = 2, p = 0.000 < 0.05
PJ * Military: F = 10.483, df = 2, p = 0.000 < 0.05

Political Elite	(N = 254)	(N = 97)	(N = 171)
War J Mean	5.21	6.03	4.69
Peace J Mean	3.05	3.31	3.25

WJ * Pol. Elite: F = 9.626, df = 2, p = 0.000 < 0.05
PJ * Pol. Elite: F = 0.748, df = 2, p = 0.474 > 0.05

Independent Experts	(N = 37)	(N = 74)	(N = 411)
War J Mean	4.27	5.22	5.27
Peace J Mean	3.57	3.28	3.11

WJ * Indep. Experts: F = 2.850, df = 2, p = 0.059 > 0.05
PJ * Indep. Experts: F = 0.938, df = 2, p = 0.392 > 0.05

Insurgents	(N = 24)	(N = 35)	(N = 463)
War J Mean	6.21	5.60	5.11
Peace J Mean	3.29	3.63	3.12

WJ * Insurgents: F = 2.869, df = 2, p = 0.058 > 0.05
PJ * Insurgents: F = 0.967, df = 2, p = 0.381 > 0.05

Civilians	(N = 83)	(N = 68)	(N = 371)
War J Mean	4.31	5.34	5.36
Peace J Mean	3.89	3.63	2.91

WJ * Civilians: F = 6.478, df = 2, p = 0.002 < 0.05
PJ * Civilians: F = 9.306, df = 2, p = 0.000 < 0.05

Note: Each type comprises several individual source-actors, as listed in Tables 5. Thus, multiple quotes by one type within a given article are possible; only the "highest" form of access by each type in each article was recorded for purposes of this table. Military comprises officers/spokespeople, and regular troops. Political Elite comprises the U.N., NATO, E.U. and other international government organizations; Karzai, Siniora, Olmert, Harper, Blair, Bush, and other heads of government, including senior former politicians; government and opposition politicians; government officials and agencies; and names countries, when used as synonyms for their governments (e.g., "Syria said…"). Independent Experts include media. Insurgents comprise Hezbollah, al-Qaida, Taliban, suicide bombers, and other anti-Western groups. Civilians also include peace activists, soldiers' families and friends, domestic and non-domestic publics and audiences, and humanitarian groups and NGOs.

without fundamentally challenging the assumptions of one's own state. Finally, our findings may be specific to the limited sample of newspapers. A parallel study by Shinar, included in this volume, finds that an Israeli tabloid's coverage of the Hezbollah conflict scored higher on most war journalism criteria than a Canadian tabloid.

One can safely conclude from our study, however, that it is possible to develop measurable criteria from PJ theory to enable cross-national and cross-conflict comparisons of news coverage. Moreover, our empirical findings, while necessarily tentative, are highly plausible. They imply that neither war journalism nor peace journalism is being consciously practiced on a wide scale, and that the prevalence of the former over the latter can be related to news organizations' structures and routines, including journalism's anchorage in the ideologies and power structures of the broader society. Oliver Boyd-Barrett (2004) argues that "war reporting" is a distinct genre that has blind spots and democratic deficiencies inscribed in its very form. We agree that war reporting does indeed have deficiencies, but in our view, these are an extension of "normal" journalism.

In the short term, our research suggests that peace journalism can be advanced obliquely by working for the reform of other aspects of news production. Of such reforms, the most important would be the broadening of the range of sources and the cultural and geographical diversification of coverage. Such shifts are unlikely to be sustained, however, without fundamental changes in the organization of journalism. These changes would likely include an ethos of responsibility rather than "objectivity" as conventionally defined; attendant shifts in the training of journalists; greater pluralism in the ownership, financing and control of major media; the development of more transnational and intercultural media organizations and of more media independent of state and private centers of power; and an enabling environment for the entrenchment and exercise of greater communication rights for ordinary people, including peacemakers. Peace journalism thus shares an agenda with emerging movements for media democratization at local, national and transnational levels.

Notes

1.   The authors acknowledge the Social Sciences and Humanities Research Council of Canada, and the vice-president of research at Simon Fraser University, for an SFU/SSHRC Institutional Grant awarded to Hackett in 2006; and a grant awarded to Dov Shinar by the Israel Association for Canadian Studies. Hackett also thanks the Toda Institute for Global Peace and Policy Research, and Toda's peace journalism research team, initially led by Dov Shinar and now by Susan Dente Ross, for their collegiality and support. For research assistance, we thank Chris Atchison, Angelika Hackett, Robert Hershorn, Chris Jeschelnik, Faiza Zia Khan, and Guoxin

Xing. The members of the NewsWatch Canada research seminar: Marie Bartlett, Jane Chan, Melissa Chungfat, Rabinder Dhillon, Faiza Zia Khan, Amanda Mc-Cuaig, Brett Robinson, Chelsea Robson, Birgitta Schroeder, Molley Zhou.

2. Arguably, our very language privileges war over peace. Authoritative dictionaries often define "peace" as "freedom from war" and "a treaty to end war"—so that peace is defined not by its positive content (such as justice) but by the absence of its opposite. Indicatively, a useful recent overview of the field is entitled *Media and Peace*, but it is mostly about wars—from Vietnam to the "War on Terror" (Spencer, 2005).

3. As the current volume attests, this approach is being developed conceptually and empirically by scholars associated with the Toda Institute for Global Peace and Policy Research and elsewhere (see e.g., Hackett, 2006; Kempf, 2003; Mandelzis, 2007; Ottosen, 2007; Peleg, 2006; Ross, 2006; Shinar, 2007; Shinar and Kempf, 2007).

4. Ranging from the micro to the macro level, they comprise media workers themselves, daily work routines, the broader organizational imperatives of media institutions, extra-media institutional influences, and ideology and cultural narratives.

5. Source: Canada. National Defence and the Canadian Forces, 2007; Washington Post Online. 2007.

6. The casualty figures differ: Reuters AlertNet (June, 2007) combines civilian and military deaths (more than 1,200 Lebanese and 157 Israeli casualties), whereas the BBC (August, 2006) states that 116 IDF soldiers and 43 Israeli civilians, and 1,109 Lebanese civilians, 28 Lebanese soldiers were killed. Hezbollah and fellow Shia militant group Amal estimate 250 Hezbollah fighters were killed, whereas the Israeli military puts the number of Hezbollah casualties at more than 530.

7. Group I looked at articles published in the *Globe and Mail*, the *Toronto Sun*, the *New York Times, and the New York Post*. These four leading English-language newspapers papers were selected on the basis of two parallel axes, enabling a comparison of both Canadian and American news perspectives, as well as of "quality" and tabloid news coverage.

    The articles were retrieved from the Lexis-Nexis and the Canadian Newsstand databases. For all four newspapers, the search terms "Hezbollah AND Israel, AND NOT business AND NOT sports" within the date range July 1 to September 1, 2006, were employed for the Israel/Hezbollah conflict. The search terms "Afghanistan AND NOT business AND NOT sports" within the same date range were used for the Afghanistan conflict.

    Group II's sample comprised articles from the Canadian *National Post*, the *Toronto Star*, and the Israeli *Jerusalem Post*. All three newspapers are broadsheet newspapers; one is liberal and locally oriented (*Toronto Star*), the other two conservative and nationally oriented.

    The articles were retrieved from Lexis-Nexis and the Canadian Newsstand databases. The search terms "Hizbullah and Israel or Afghanistan and Taliban not SECTION business and sports" were used for Lexis-Nexis, and "Hezbollah and Israel or Afghanistan and Taliban (in CITATION AND DOCUMENT TEXT) AND NOT business and sports (in SECTION)" for the Canadian Newsstand database. The same date range, July 1 – September 1, 2006 was employed for all searches.

8. The following search strings were employed: "Afghanistan," "Israel," "Lebanon or Hezbollah or Hizbullah" were individually entered in the search engines provided by the news outlet. Articles from the *Jerusalem Post* were retrieved from Lexis-Nexis with the following search string: (Afghanistan or (Lebanon or (Hizbullah or Hezbollah)).

9.   Although the original intent was to consider both conflicts, Group II experienced inconsistency in the data collection process and their searches resulted in little to no articles related to the Afghanistan conflict. Consequently, Group II chose to drop the topic and focused solely on the Israel-Lebanon conflict.

10.   We used this definition to exclude peripheral articles: The conflict has to be mentioned in either the headline or in the beginning of the story (first 200 words or first five paragraphs). If the conflict is not mentioned in the headline but in the beginning of the story, the rest of the article has to talk further about the conflict. If neither conflict is mentioned in the headlines or beyond a single paragraph of the article, then exclude it from the sample even if the reference to either conflict occurs within the first five paragraphs of the story.

11.   The *Jerusalem Post* online only archives articles that are published in its print version. Thus, articles from the *Jerusalem Post* were retrieved from the Lexis-Nexis database.

12.   Al-Jazeera was selected to allow comparison of conflict coverage between publications from countries that are directly involved in armed conflict versus news coverage from a country that is not directly involved, and that reflects an Arab rather than a Western perspective.

13.   A constructed week consists of a random draw to amass a full seven days worth of articles from the original nine-week timeframe.

Constructed Week Dates:

	Group I Dates	*Group II* Dates
Monday	July 3, 2006	August 28, 2006
Tuesday	August 15, 2006	July 18, 2006
Wednesday	July 26, 2006	August 2, 2006
Thursday	July 20, 2006	July 27, 2006
Friday	August 25, 2006	July 14, 2006
Saturday	August 5, 2006	July 8, 2006
Sunday	August 27, 2006	August 13, 2006

In order to provide an equal opportunity for articles from each of the publications to be selected, for any publication that was not published on a weekend date (i.e., Saturday or Sunday), articles were extracted on the next date of publication, after the selected date.

14.   A story is *zero-sum* oriented when the conflict is not only described as two-sided, but also as a relationship in which any gain for one side is a loss for the other. In Peace Journalism zero-sum orientation is described as being "a simple question of geometry. Two points can only be joined in one way—with a line. This means that any change in the relations between them can only take place along a single axis. The conflict becomes a tug of war.... It's a "zero-sum game," in which each party ultimately faces only two possibilities, victory or defeat. Peace = victory + ceasefire" (Lynch and McGoldrick, 2005a: 6-8, and 42-47).

15.   *Supportive of "our" role*: i.e., the position of the country in which the news outlet is produced.

16.   *Invisible effects of war* such as long-term economic costs, political reputations, the "cultural capital" of hope and trust.

17.   A story is considered to be *people-oriented* if it gives voice to all parties; empathy and understanding are the focus. (Lynch and McGoldrick, 2005a: 6).

18.   *Structural violence* is usually understood as a system of political, social or economic relations, that creates barriers that people cannot remove—barriers to at-

taining food, shelter, education, jobs, security, etc. It may take visible forms such as "whites-only" busses in Apartheid South Africa, but it is usually thought of as an invisible form of violence, built into ways of doing and ways of thinking. (Lynch and McGoldrick, 2005a: 59). Includes poverty, racism, systematic denial of human rights, repression of women, etc.

Cultural violence means cultural forms that justify or glorify violence. But it exists as ideas and images carried in people's minds so that it, too, is usually thought of as an invisible form of violence. It includes speech, persecution, myths and legends of war heroes, religious justifications for violence or war, the idea that one group of people are the chosen people, and civilizational arrogance (pp. 59-60).

19. Describes the many goals and issues, and is solution-oriented. It reports on alternatives to zero-sum perspective. Also includes articles that emphasize how war/failure to make peace costs both sides, and/or that suggest that war itself, rather than a particular group or regime, is the problem.

20. A copy of the codebook and comment section detailing individual coder's procedures and decisions regarding anomalies, as well as the results of all inter-coder reliability tests from all three groups are available upon request.

21. The PJ indicator scale ranges from 0-10 (score 10 denoting "ideal" conditions), with a mean of 3.16 with a standard deviation of 2.13 and Cronbach's Alpha = 0.629 (N=522). A mean of 3.21, with a standard deviation of 2.16 and Cronbach's Alpha = 0.626 resulted from the sample excluding the "Lebanon-only" sub-sample (n=323) only. The WJ index also ranges from 0-10 with a mean of 5.19 with a standard deviation of 2.45 and Cronbach's Alpha = 0.673 (N=522). And a mean of 5.59, with a standard deviation of 2.46 and Cronbach's Alpha = 0.676 resulted from the sample looking at the Afghan sub-sample (n= 323) only.

References

Allan, Stuart, and Zelizer, Barbie, (eds.). 2004. *Reporting War: Journalism in Wartime.* London and New York: Routledge.

BBC Online. 2006. "Middle East crisis: Facts and figures." Published August 21, 2006 at http://news.bbc.co.uk/2/hi/middle_east/5257128.stm.

Bennett, Lance, W., and Paletz, David, L. 1994. *Taken by Storm: The media, public opinion, and U.S. foreign policy in the Gulf War.* Chicago: University of Chicago Press.

Boyd-Barrett, Oliver. 2004. "Understanding: The Second Casualty," in S. Allan and B. Zelizer (eds.), *Reporting War: Journalism in Wartime.* London and New York: Routledge, pp. 25-42.

Canada. National Defence and the Canadian Forces, 2007. "Fallen Canadians." Available from: http://www.forces.gc.ca/site/focus/fallen/index_e.asp.

Hackett, Robert, A. 2007. "Journalism versus peace? Notes on a problematic relationship." *Global Media Journal: Mediterranean Edition* 2(1): 47-53.

Hackett, Robert, A. 2006. "Is peace journalism possible? Three frameworks for assessing structure and agency in news media." *Conflict and Communication Online*, 5(2). Available at: www.cco.regener-online.de.

Hackett, Robert, A. 1989. "Coups, Earthquakes and Hostages? Foreign news on Canadian television." *Canadian Journal of Political Science* 22(4): 809-825.

Hackett, Robert, A., and Carroll, William, K. 2006. *Remaking Media: The struggle to democratize public communication.* London: Routledge.

Hackett, Robert A., and Zhao, Yuezhi. 1998. *Sustaining Democracy? Journalism and the politics of objectivity.* Toronto: Garamond.

Hanitzsch, Thomas. 2004. "Journalists as peacekeeping force? Peace journalism and mass communication theory." *Journalism Studies* 5 (4): 483-95.

Kellner, Douglas. 1992. *The Persian Gulf TV War.* Boulder: Westview Press.

Kempf, Wilhelm. 2003. "Constructive conflict coverage: A social-psychological research and development program," in *Conflict and Communication Online*, 2 (2). Available at: www.cco.regener-online.de.

Klopfenstein, Bruce. 2006. "Terrorism and the exploitation of new media," in Anandam P. Kavoori and Todd Fraley (eds.), *Media, Terrorism, and Theory.* Lanham: Rowman & Littlefield, pp. 107-20.

Knightley, Philip. 2000. "War journalism under fire." Committee for Peace in the Balkans. Available at: http://www.peaceinbalkans.freeserve.co.uk.

Liebes, Tamar, and Kampf, Zohar. 2004. "The PR of terror: how new-style wars give voice to terrorists," in Stuart Allan and Barbie Zelizer (eds.), *Reporting War: Journalism in Wartime.* London and New York: Routledge, pp. 77-95.

Lynch, Jake. 2006. "What's so great about peace journalism?" *Global Media Journal: Mediterranean Edition* 1(1): 74-87. Available from: http://globalmedia.emu.edu.tr/spring2006/inagural_issues/7.%20Jake%20Lynch%20Whats%20so%20great%20about2.pdf .

Lynch, Jake, and McGoldrick, Annabel. 2005a. *Peace Journalism.* Stroud, U.K.: Hawthorn Press.

Lynch, Jake, and McGoldrick, Annabel. 2005b. "Peace journalism: A global dialog for democracy and democratic media," in Robert A. Hackett and Yuezhi Zhao (eds.), *Democratizing Global Media: One world, many struggles*, Lanham MD: Rowman and Littlefield, pp. 269-88.

Mandelzis, Lea. 2007. "Representations of Peace in News Discourse: Viewpoint and Opportunity for Peace Journalism." *Conflict and Communication Online*, 6(1). Available at: www.cco.regener-online.de.

Maslog, Crispin C., Lee, Seow Ting, and Kim, Hun Shik. 2006. "Framing analysis of a conflict: How newspapers in five Asian countries covered the Iraq war," in *Asian Journal of Communication* 16 (1): 19-39.

McChesney, Robert W. 2004. *The Problem of the Media: U.S. Communication Politics in the Twenty-first Century.* New York: Monthly Review Press.

Mowlana, Hamid, Gerbner, George, and Schiller, Herbert I. 1992. *Triumph of the Image: The media's war in the Persian Gulf—a global perspective.* Boulder: Westview Press.

Muravchik, Joshua. 2003. *Covering the Intifada: How the media reported the Palestinian uprising.* Washington: The Washington Institute for Near East Policy.

Ottosen, Rune. 2007. "Emphasising Images in Peace Journalism: Theory and Practice in the Case of Norway's Biggest Newspaper," in *Conflict & Communication Online*, 6 (1). Available at: www.cco.regener-online.de.

Peleg, Samuel. 2006. "Peace Journalism through the Lens of Conflict Theory: Analysis and Practice." in *Conflict and Communication Online*, 5(2). Available at: www.cco.regener-online.de.

Philo, Greg, and Berry, Mike. 2004. *Bad News from Israel.* London: Pluto Press.

Reuters AlertNet Online. 2007. "Lebanon crisis. Timeline." Available at: http://www.alertnet.org/db/crisisprofiles/LB_CRI.htm?v=timeline.

Ricchiardi, Sherry. 2006. "The Forgotten War," in *American Journalism Review,* August/September 2006. Available at: http://www.ajr.org/Article.asp?id=4162.

Ross, Susan Dente. 2006. "(De)Constructing Conflict: A Focused Review of War and Peace Journalism," in *Conflict and Communication Online* 5 (2). Available at: www.cco.regener-online.de.

Shinar, Dov. 2007. "Peace journalism: The state of the art," in *Conflict and Communication Online* 6 (1). Available at: www.cco.regener-online.de.

Shinar, Dov, and Kempf, Wilhelm (eds.). 2007. *Peace Journalism: The State of the Art.* Berlin: Verlag Irena Regener.

Shoemaker, Pamela, and Reese, Stephen D. 1996. *Mediating the Message: Theories of influences on mass media content* (2nd edition). White Plains, NY: Longman.

Spencer, Graham. 2005. *The Media and Peace: From Vietnam to the "War on Terror."* New York: Palgrave Macmillan.

Tehranian, Majid. 2002. "Peace Journalism: Negotiating global media ethics," in *Harvard International Journal of Press/Politics* 7(2) (April): 58-83.

Tuchman, Gaye. 1978. *Making news: A study in the construction of reality.* New York: Free Press/Macmillan.

Washington Post Online. 2007. "Faces of the Fallen." Available at http://projects.washingtonpost.com/fallen/.

Wolfsfeld, Gadi. 2004. *Media and the path to peace.* Cambridge. Cambridge University Press.

A Summer's Pastime: Strategic Construction of the 2006 War in Lebanon

Susan Dente Ross[1]

Introduction

This study of U.S. newspaper coverage of the 2006 war in Lebanon is part of the continuing project of peace journalism scholars to develop a more complete understanding of the nature of mainstream "war journalism" as a point of departure for adaptation and alteration of news reporting norms. Accordingly, this research is grounded in Johan Galtung's (1998) initiative to criticize *and alter* the professional values and techniques that lead mainstream news production to favor war, violence, and the agenda of elites (Kempf, 2001; Lynch and Mc-Goldrick, 2005).

This work also builds upon the significant literature in "framing" that suggests, but does not fully elaborate, how news frames—e.g., thematically linked discursive representations of ideas, actors and events—"define and construct political issues and controversies" in ways that reflect and perpetuate the elite norms and values of dominant cultures (Nelson, Clawson, and Oxley, 1997). News norms that guide the selection and highlighting of information establish stable frames and representations in ways that narrow the reasonable attribution of blame, definition of victims, and identification of problem solutions (Entman, 1993, 2004; Iyengar, 1990, 1991).

Finally, this study seeks to bring together the critical perspectives elaborated in news framing studies with an understanding of the exacerbating impact of news "waves" to clarify further some professionally embedded points of resistance to peace journalism practices. Berkowitz (1992) identified news waves as the routine increase in both the amount and intensity of media coverage tied to "key" events that attract journalists' attention (Brosius and Eps, 1995; Cobb and Elder,

1972; Kepplinger and Habermier, 1995; Wolfsfeld, 2001). Political actors who routinely dominate the news trigger waves of media attention highly integrated with government initiatives, priorities, perspectives and policies (Wolfsfeld and Sheafer, 2006). At the same time, "an individual or group who is part of the formal political establishment" can prompt a news wave by breaking ranks and diverging from the official ideology or "group speak" (Wolfsfeld and Sheafer, 2006).

Wolfsfeld and Shearer (2006) suggested that news waves generated through government initiative, enterprise reporting or outsider challenges to the elite-dominated status quo significantly affect both the nature and quantity of news coverage. Even when coverage waves are dominated by the familiar voices of power, the increased quantity of news reporting may require journalists to broaden the range of acceptable journalistic sources. Scholars have argued that news waves force reporters to "search hard for relevant information" and unearth previously unexposed perspectives and sources on the news (Brosius and Epps, 1995).

This study seeks to examine whether the inclusion of new voices and more diverse information during waves of coverage may lead mainstream journalists toward some elements of peace journalism practice (see, e.g., Bennett, 1990, 1996; Mandelzis, 2003; Ross and Bantimaroudis, 2006; Wolfsfeld and Sheafer, 2006). In particular, this study of newspaper content explores whether the wave of coverage of a distant international war increased the variety of sources of news and whether changes in the quantity of news coverage also altered the nature of the reporting.

This study seeks to answer several specific research questions. First, did the wave of news coverage of the 2006 war in Lebanon lead journalists to use a greater diversity of non-elite sources in their reporting? Second, did the wave of coverage change the nature of coverage of the nations and peoples involved in the war? Third, to what degree did any identified shifts in coverage move coverage away from the explicit policies and priorities of the official U.S. elite position? Finally, did any identified shifts in coverage move reporting toward peace journalism practices?

Method

This study employed qualitative content analysis of all of the coverage (news, columns, editorials, etc.) of the 2006 war in Lebanon in *The*

Seattle Times between mid-June and mid-September 2006. *The Seattle Times* is a mid-sized metropolitan daily serving the largest city in the Pacific Northwest of the United States, delivering nearly 235,000 papers daily. While much research on U.S. newspapers focuses on elite news organizations (e.g., *The New York Times*), this study set out to examine the content of a "typical" U.S. newspaper. The intent is to identify the news content in the type of newspaper most likely to reach an average newspaper reader in the United States as distinguished from news aimed at a national or international audience.[2, 3]

An online search of the full-text version of *The Seattle Times* identified 170 items including the terms "Lebanon" and "Israel" during 2006. The distribution of stories throughout the year demonstrated a "wave" of news coverage (nearly 60 percent of the year's coverage) between June and September. The author scanned all 98 items printed during this four-month period to identify the 84 texts related to the war in Lebanon, which were heavily concentrated between July and mid-September. The limited duration of the 34-day war between Israel and Lebanon and the nearly total absence of U.S. news coverage of Hezbollah (and, indeed, Lebanon) before and after the conflict created an exemplary case in which to apply deep qualitative analysis to an entire wave of news coverage to identify shifts in the nature of coverage during a news wave.

The author read the entire wave of coverage in depth several times, using inductive analysis to build from specific examples to categorical understandings of the content. Categories emerged from patterns observed in the coverage based on the researcher's tacit knowledge of the professional norms and practices of U.S. newspapers and the political, social and economic context of the war. The power of this qualitative analysis relies not on statistical significance but rather on the rich understanding of the researcher, which is informed by extensive professional media experience and ongoing scholarship in mass communication, media studies and intercultural communication. Through the process of deep reading, the author identified four distinct phases of news coverage of the war as, consecutively, the elite perspective dominated, came under challenge and then re-established its dominance.

In the discussion that follows, I call the first phase of coverage: "Look Here!" During this onset of news coverage, the official discourse of Western elites dominated reports in which the war was represented as a component of a broader strategy to eradicate terrorism. A second coverage phase, dubbed "Who's Right?" emerged as the wave of coverage peaked and news texts incorporated growing disagreement among the Western elite partners over the proper execution of the war, the acceptable humanitarian costs, and even the identity of the "enemy." During this coverage phase, increasing expression of Lebanese and Israeli discontent provided a variety of frames for understanding the war, the players, and the objectives. Challenges to the Western representation of the war were subsequently overcome or eliminated by a return to elite-dominated discussion of a cease-fire agreement that "resolved" the "problem" in Lebanon. This "Resolution" phase incorporated a more limited diversity of sources and perspectives than the previous phase. During the final coverage phase, which I call "Look Away," the now-dominant Western elite sources no longer focused their attention or comments on Lebanon, and the topic quickly disappeared from the news, as the wave of coverage subsided.

Findings

Waves of Attention and Inattention

Coverage of what came to be known as "the summer's 34-day war" in Lebanon (Mideast Digest, *Seattle Times*, October 21, 2006) typifies the waves of news reporting identified by numerous scholars. In the weeks prior to July 14, 2006, the term "Hezbollah" did not appear at all in the pages of *The Seattle Times*. The newspaper's readers heard virtually nothing about Lebanon in the first six months of the year before Hezbollah burst into the headlines and appeared in an average of one or two stories a day between mid-July and mid-September. The peak of the coverage wave occurred in late July, with a shooting at a Seattle Jewish center, and in-mid August as the United Nations brokered a cease-fire agreement. News roundups and letters to the editor, rather than full-length reports on the conflict, played a prominent role in both early and late mentions of Hezbollah and represented a significant thread of the 84 stories that created a three-month wave of coverage before both Hezbollah and Lebanon again essentially disappeared from the newspaper.

This "burst" of attention, devoid of foundation and detached from context, paralleled and reinforced narratives that, as one reader suggested, caused both Arab and Israeli "partisans [to see] bias [because] each wanted more context" (Large, It stands to reason, *Seattle Times*, August 10, 2006). Moreover, the abrupt end of the coverage wave removed significant political, military and policy issues from the public view without closure or attention to underlying causes. A closer examination of the news wave identified the following four phases of coverage.

Phase I: Look Here! The Antiterrorism Initiative, July 12-25, 2006

The first mention of Hezbollah and the first coverage of the war in *The Seattle Times* laid full blame for the conflict at the feet of the Shiite Muslim terrorists (Hezbollah), established Israel as the victim, and justified U.S.-backed Israeli military offensives as necessary and defensive (Mideast fighting, 2006). Early stories, relying predominately

Figure 1
Construction of the Lebanon "Summer" War

Phases of Coverage

Table 1

	Stories/100 day	% West Elite	% Hezbollah & friends	% US citizens
Look Here!	143	55	10	40
Who's Right?	180	47	33	31
Resolution	108	62	39	23
Look Away!	28	12	18	24

on government and military officials, clearly established the single and proximate cause of the conflict as Hezbollah's kidnapping of two Israeli soldiers and killing of eight others (The Eye-catchers, 2006). The texts made equally clear and unequivocal the proper response—to "cripple" Hezbollah (Mideast fighting, 2006; Nissenbaum, July 23, 2006).

The omniscient narrator of most news coverage of the 34-day war echoed Bush administration perspectives and supported Israeli actions as an essential component of the global war on terror (see, e.g., Nissenbaum and Strobel, July 22, 2006). Early *Seattle Times* reports were dominated by statements from representatives of the United States and its core friends—the European Union, some human rights groups, Israel, and select (generally conservative, pro-military) policy analysts. Israeli and other voices aligned with U.S. or Western ideologies were presented as the bearers of truth, creating the foundational presuppositions (to adopt Van Dijk's terminology) that framed the war.

In this liberation narrative, the United States and its "first friend," Israel, were working alongside the "weak" Lebanese army to protect and support the "fragile, young" democratic government of Lebanon and free its people from terrorism (Nissenbaum and Strobel, July 22, 2006; Nissenbaum, July 23, 2006; Fryer, Cantwell, McGavick, July 28, 2006). Israeli offensive military strikes were framed as "retaliation," and the war was Israel's "second front" against Muslim fanaticism and anti-Semitism (Hsu and King, 2006; Nissenbaum, July 18, 2006; Nissenbaum, July 23, 2006). The dominant narrative presented the war as a battle for freedom, the vital "groundwork for peace." In the words of Secretary of State Condoleezza Rice, for example, the war should be understood as the initial "birth pangs of a new Middle East" (Nissenbaum and Strobel, July 22, 2006).

Through these narratives, U.S. and Israeli officials articulated a ready-made and easily accessible heuristic of Hezbollah as a rogue element, the forefront of radical, terrorist Muslim fanaticism. In this discourse, Hezbollah existed only in the present, as a proxy, a puppet "backed by Syria and Iran." One rare historical account explained Hezbollah's emergence and ascendancy in Lebanon as an Iranian initiative to repel Israel's 1982 invasion of Lebanon (Mideast fighting, July 14, 2006). In stark contrast with the homegrown "resistance movement" they proclaimed themselves to be, Hezbollah members and their supporters were presented as the leading "subcontractors for the axis of evil," subverting the legitimate Lebanese government and attacking the United States and its allies (Mideast fighting, July 14, 2006; Nissenbaum, July 18, 2006).

Yet even in the opening days of the war, the discourse of preventative military offensive action was not seamless. Passing references, often buried deep within narratives of war as the path to peace, described Hezbollah as a complex and multifaceted organization with deep interconnections with the people of Lebanon. Here readers might learn that it was Hezbollah, not the Lebanese army, which previously had "fought an 18-year guerrilla war to force Israel to withdraw from southern Lebanon" (Mideast fighting, July 14, 2006). Occasional mentions of Hezbollah's popularity and good deeds—e.g., it "runs TV and radio stations, a weekly newspaper and an Internet site ... [and provides] schools, hospitals, dental clinics, and drinking water" in regions where the Lebanese government is absent or ineffectual—presented these activities as strategic and subversive, designed to disguise the organization's true mission and to dupe the Lebanese people (Mideast fighting, July 14, 2006).

The Lebanese government, the putative partner to Western military actions against Hezbollah, was largely silent or shunned in news narratives of the opening days of the fighting. For example, when, after less than a week of fighting, "Lebanon's prime minister pleaded for a cease-fire," he was flatly rebuffed by Israel and the United States (Nissenbaum, July 18, 2006). Only after the fighting lingered, and the Israeli "operation" failed to remove Hezbollah neatly and efficiently from southern Lebanon, did the Western discourse of "might makes right" begin to come under challenge.

At first, such challenges were buried or half-voiced. Fleeting critiques of Western intervention in Lebanon appeared occasionally late in news texts, almost as asides, and in opinion pieces. In one such critique, half way through a long story focused on Israeli military strategy, the omniscient narrator noted that Israel's efforts to destabilize Hezbollah "appeared to be destabilizing the Lebanese government," an apparently unintended and undesired side effect (Nissenbaum and Strobel, July 22, 2006). With reports of growing "collateral damage" of devastation and carnage, the news noted that many Israeli civilians had begun to equate the war with Israel's previous "costly 17-year military campaign in Lebanon ... their nation's Vietnam." News stories also mentioned the cost, largely in terms of international opinion, to the United States for its strong support of Israel's intervention and noted how the United States had been "sucked into Lebanon's civil war" in the '80s, resulting in the destruction of the U.S. "Marine barracks in Beirut, killing 241 Marines" (Nissenbaum, July 18, 2006).

In the early days of the conflict, when some of the news accounts dominated by Israeli and U.S. sources reported "a refugee crisis" in

Lebanon, where "mostly civilians have been killed," a whiff of censor-ship appeared, with Israel intentionally "targeting Arab and foreign media" (Nissenbaum, July 23, 2006). Such critiques of U.S./Israeli actions generally were drowned out by a narrative that naturalized the military violence as a political strategy and a path to peace. The military was cast as the benevolent savior whose self-sacrifice should be understood as necessary, and whose acts of destruction should be seen as defensive. For Israel, then, "a one-sided war where the other team gets to plan how to kill us and we get to talk is nuts" (Nissenbaum and Strobel, July 22, 2006).

By the second week of the war, Lebanese government officials oc-casionally directly rejected the Western liberation tale. One Lebanese minister said the "Lebanese military was prepared to fight Israeli troops if they crossed into his country. 'The army did not attack Israel, but if there is a ground offensive, then orders given to the army will be to defend themselves' " (Nissenbaum and Strobel, July 22, 2006). At the same time, voices of alarm and opposition to the war began to emerge from U.S. sources. In one story, Newt Gingrich equated "violence in Israel and Lebanon [with] evidence of World War III" (Postman, July 16, 2006). In another, Condoleezza Rice said "work for peace will be difficult" (Nissenbaum and Strobel, July 22, 2006).

The voices of Lebanese and U.S. citizens also began to enter the news and to bring pieces of a narrative of humanitarian loss, to tell the tale of the destruction and pain (Nissenbaum, July 23, 2006).

> More than half a million residents have fled their homes, with more then 140,000 seeking refuge in Syria. The Israeli bombardment has devastated major roads, bridges, villages, neighborhoods and Beirut's airport. Nearly a third of the 350 people who've been killed in the attacks have been children (Nissenbaum and Strobel, July 22, 2006).

Opinion columns and letters to the editor tended to present the most extreme views and the greatest alarm. In one piece, titled "an endless summer," the author challenged the foresight and power of the West, saying the conflict was "toxic with unintended consequences" (Gaza and Lebanon, 2006). A letter writer feared "something worse will happen" (Diamond, 2006). From citizens both vehemently supporting and oppos-ing Israel's actions, the conflict was viewed as a counterproductive and unwinnable "calamity," "sow[ing] the seeds for years of more misery," and U.S. policy in the war was "cynical," self-serving and unjust (Give a green light, 2006; Dunn, 2006; Harkavy, 2006; Marsh, 2006). One writer summarized the opinions of many: Even given the utter idiocy of Hezbollah's actions, Israel's response ... shows no regard or respect for human lives and dignity. The campaign it is conducting against Lebanon is ... not directed against Hezbollah, but against the entire country, killing and maiming at will. [The result will be the] destruction of the one secular, democratic government in the Middle East (Hulays, 2006).

Another writer said the fighting could not achieve its objectives because it could not address the "real political differences" at issue (Give a green light, 2006). Many writers decried what one called the "collapse of moral order ... just on the horizon" (Osawa, 2006).

Phase II: Who's Right? Lebanon's Challenge to the West, July 26-August 14, 2006

As the war turned toward its third week, letters to the editor in *The Seattle Times* conveyed the breadth of opinion and the depth of emotion connected with the war. Encapsulated in the mounting flurry of letters were increasingly charged language and more fixed and confrontational positions. Many writers blamed Hezbollah solely and entirely for the conflict. One wrote, "When Israel responds in a move to root out this threat, Hezbollah makes human shields of Lebanese civilians to maximize civilian deaths ... [and the] Iranian ... solution is just destroy Israel" (Hanson, 2006). Another writer noted that "Israel has never historically been the aggressor, but has been in a position of defending itself since ... forever" (Extract, 2006). In the rhetoric of mutual polarization and demonization, pro-Israeli voices dominated. "Hezbollah or Hamas ... deliberately target without any warning children and civilians [while] Israel takes pains to warn civilians ... [and] at least tries to avoid hitting civilians." While "Israel attacks strategic and military targets; its enemy attacks children and civilians" (Extract, 2006).

One writer condemned Hezbollah as an organization without conscience that "hide[s] among innocents" with "no compunction or desire to fight or act honorably" (Goodstein, 2006). Another railed against "the unwashed feet of Hezbollah, [which] ... fights, hides and operates in civilian areas to use [civilians] as a shield" and said the international dismantling of this "terrorist organization ... will result in a safer world for all of us" (Hawkins, 2006). One author also castigated those who would criticize Israel's response to Hezbollah's "unprovoked" attack "across a recognized international border" (Hanson, 2006), while another asked "who upbraids Hezbollah or Hamas when they deliberately target without any warning children and civilians?" (Extract, 2006).

While these statements presented a mounting challenge to the construction of the war as reasonable and effective, relatively rare (but nonetheless present) letters offered direct critique of Israeli-Western actions. Letters overtly challenged the Western representation of the war and argued that "the current situation is a political issue disguised as a religious one. The conflict has roots in politics and power," not terrorism (Rahman, 2006). Others directly challenged the dominant representation of Israel as unequivocally good and Hezbollah as an externally funded terrorist organization bent on religious supremacy. Thus, one reader criticized the nature of Israel's response: "Hezbollah began this war on Israel's northern border [but that] ... simply doesn't justify the wholesale destruction of an entire nation [or] ... the callous, cynical disregard for life that Israel and its lobbyists have adopted. To put it simply, Israel is not the victim, it is the bully" (Walsh, 2006). Another also challenged Israel's position as respondent, "Israeli ... generals are declaring that Hezbollah is 'a cancer' and must be eliminated ... But since the members of Hezbollah are Lebanese, and Israelis are the invaders, this strikes me as a case of the tumor accusing the body of being the 'disease' " (Browne Jr., 2006).

Antipathy toward the conflict itself, rather than to either the Israelis or Hezbollah, became more evident in news stories as the war toll mounted and Israeli success appeared increasingly uncertain. In the second phase of coverage, accounts that validated Israel's military objectives and "right to self-defense" also incorporated detailed reports of mounting humanitarian harm told from the Lebanese perspective (Nissenbaum, July 23, 2006). A growing number of stories included an expanding range of voices that recounted the Israeli public's discontent with the war and presented Hezbollah, Lebanese and Israeli reactions to the conflict on a more equal basis (see, e.g., Bengali and Nissenbaum, August 13, 2006).

Although Lebanese perspectives remained primarily in discrete stories focused on criticisms of Israeli atrocities or rising reactionary extremism against Israel and the United States, Lebanese civilians gained power to speak for themselves and to mourn their dead (see, e.g., Allam, July 31, 2006; Bazzi, August 2, 2006; Fadel, August 7, 2006; Fadel, August 11, 2006). In this second coverage phase, detailed reports such as news of the Israeli massacre in Qana, with its "stench of death" and "assembly line" that "dumped rotting bodies ... of dead children" into a mass grave stood juxtaposed with "fact-based" accounts of war strategy to provide a context for resistive decoding of the U.S.-Israeli commentary on the transformation of Lebanon into the "new breeding ground for guerrilla fighters" and Islamic fundamentalist terrorism (Nissenbaum and Strobel,

July 22, 2006; Nissenbaum, August 3, 2006). Voices of Muslim Americans similarly remained in discrete content apart from the mainstream of coverage (see, e.g., Mullin, August 10, 2006; August 12, 2006), but the composite news content included challenges to the Western hegemonic perspective on the war.

During this period, the composite narrative—taken as a whole—offered a dialogic network among citizen letters, narratives told from the Arab or Muslim perspective, and news accounts that began to offer a counterpoint between Western positions and those of the people of Lebanon. This web of interactive texts opened discursive terrain for a more varied and complex portrait of Hezbollah to emerge, such that accounts of the Iranian-backed "rebel" group played against stories of "resistance" fighters repelling "Israeli aggression" (Nissenbaum and Strobel, July 22, 2006; Allam, July 31, 2006; Nissenbaum, August 3, 2006; Bengali and Nissenbaum, August 13, 2006). Through these narratives, Hezbollah was presented, concurrently, as a religiously fanatic militia and a legitimate, popular political group fighting alongside and reinforcing the Lebanese army (Nissenbaum, August 3, 2006; Bengali and Strobel, U.S., France join in cease-fire call in Lebanon war, *Seattle Times*, August 6, 2006; Nissenbaum and Strobel, August 12, 2006; Bengali and Nissenbaum, August 13, 2006; Rosenberg and Fadel, August 13, 2006).

This dialogic debate afforded the Lebanese government the opportunity to separate itself, its people and its goals from those of the West. Increased textual allusions to Israel's prior invasion of Lebanon called up the continuing bitter aftermath of the earlier war (Bazzi, August 2, 2006; Bengali and Strobel, August 6, 2006). Lebanese citizens and government officials increasingly spoke for themselves to express anger about being "deserted by America," the former "friend and protector" of the Lebanese (Fadel, August 11, 2006). The new voices in the news blamed the United States, which "blindly support[s] Israel," for the war (Bazzi, August 2, 2006). In these texts, U.S.-Israeli military aggression had prompted both an increasingly unified Lebanese "resistance" against "the Israeli enemy [who] has no mercy for anybody" and "newfound support of Hezbollah militancy" to free Lebanon from the invaders (Fadel, August 7, 2006). The war, initially framed as an opportunity for the West to liberate Lebanon from terrorism, now was also presented as a "crisis [that] … has the potential to create far more terrorists who can threaten both Israel and the West" (Jeffers, August 9, 2006).

Events also began to fracture the Israeli-U.S. official narrative on the war. In the wake of a Hezbollah rocket attack in northern Israel, the "images of wounded soldiers carried off helicopters raised haunting memories of Israel's 18-year occupation of southern Lebanon" (Losses leaving, July 27, 2006; Nissenbaum, August 7, 2006). Stories that opened with "images" of wounded "pajama-clad children" and reports of targeted Israeli attacks on "Lebanon's largest Palestinian refugee camp" undermined the credibility of Israeli claims that their actions constituted a "justified," "self-defensive" and "reasonable response" (Nissenbaum, August 3, 2006; Israel replaces, August 9, 2006; Nissenbaum and Strobel, August 12, 2006). The human costs on both sides became increasingly apparent in texts that included the stories of citizens alongside those of military officers.

As the narrative of Israeli victimization began to crumble, some stories used passive voice and other means to obscure the cause of the war. Rather than locate the cause of an increasingly unpopular war in the "hostage crisis alone," texts began to simply report that the "war broke out" (Bazzi, August 2, 2006). The ambiguous causation provided cover for Israeli officials to re-frame a war that was costing mounting Israeli losses as a proportionate response to "a threat to our nation" (Bengali and Nissenbaum, August 13, 2006). Increasing erasure of responsibility and bureaucratization of the war presented the plight of Lebanese refugees and wounded civilians as an account of a "demographic shift [that] will take months, probably years, to sort out" (Allam, July 30, 2006).

At the same time, Western initiatives to broker a cease-fire provided an opportunity for official U.S.-Israeli spokespeople to reclaim the discursive terrain and overcome rising challenges to their hegemony. Despite pleas for a cease-fire from the Lebanese prime minister within days of the initial Israeli attacks, the "cease-fire" proposals that emerged in early August were solely a project of the West that sought to impose peace on "the warring parties" (Long, August 6, 2006; Bengali and Strobel, August 6, 2006; Rosenberg and Fadel, August 13, 2006).

The cease-fire endorsed by the United States prompted the largest burst of news coverage of the war, drawing attention back to Western officials and away from the reality on the ground, which included Israel's most aggressive military push of the war. With news narratives focused on U.N. representatives brokering an externally crafted cease-fire, Israel's "tripled ... troop strength," "stepped up ... airstrikes," and most aggressive troop incursion deep into Lebanese territory became little more than a discursive aside (Nissenbaum and Strobel, August 12, 2006; Rosenberg and Fadel, August 13, 2006).

Despite news focus on the cease-fire, its actual terms were rarely, if ever, reported. Instead, officials constructed the cease-fire in their own terms. In one case, U.S. Secretary of State Condoleezza Rice matter-of-factly described a cease-fire in which firing would not cease: "No one can expect an immediate end to all acts of violence," she said. Instead, Israel was "expected to press ahead in an effort to *do as much as it can to cripple Hezbollah* before the cease-fire takes hold" (Nissenbaum and Strobel, August 12, 2006, emphasis added).

Phase III: Resolution, The End of Fighting, August 15-31, 2006

In the context of perceived *carte blanche* approval from the United States, and within rapidly diminishing news coverage of the war in Lebanon, Israel's position framed the discursive construction of cessation of fighting. During this third phase of declining coverage, Israeli military and government elites dominated the content and consistently asserted that the U.N. agreement allowed them to continue to occupy Lebanon until Hezbollah had been fully disarmed. As the West reclaimed its position of narrative supremacy, these and other Israeli claims assumed a ring of facticity (see, e.g., U.N. chief August 29, 2006; Fadel, September 1, 2006; Strobel and Landay, September 11, 2006). In some stories, Israel spoke alone, as if representing all sides of all issues (U.N. chief tries to bolster, August 29, 2006). Lebanese officials and citizens and representatives of Hezbollah found little room to express their views or perspectives within the dwindling volume of *Seattle Times* coverage. It was Israeli voices, therefore, that largely defined the positions of the various parties, the nature of the conflict, and the terms of the cease-fire.

In these texts, the war became merely a "border conflict" and the product "of a two-decade, Iranian-nurtured program" of aggression against Israel (Rosenberg, With Iran's help, August 20, 2006). The language of blaming Hezbollah returned, with a focus on their "snatch [of] Israeli soldiers" as *the* event "that touched off the most recent fighting" (Bengali, Hezbollah's weapons cache, August 16, 2006). Texts in the third phase of coverage also buried news of Israel transgressions deep inside stories, such as the late parenthetical mentions of Israel's "immoral" use of cluster bombs (Fadel, Cluster bombs, September 1, 2006; Europe commits troops, August 26, 2006), or the challenge to the cease-fire presented by "an Israeli commando raid" (Allam and Fadel, Lebanon demands Hezbollah, August 21, 2006). Tales of Hezbollah militancy, aggression and violence also overshadowed cursory mention of Israel's failure to achieve its military objectives (Bengali and Nissenbaum, Israel falls short of its objectives, August 13, 2006).

The silencing and undermining of Hezbollah and other perspectives challenging the Western ideology occurred both within the texts and through the withdrawal of news coverage of the war. References to Hezbollah as guerrillas and militia and militants returned in force and with greater impact given the reduced volume of coverage (Will cease-fire endure? August 15, 2006; Bengali, Hezbollah's weapons cache, August 16, 2006; Allam and Fadel, Lebanon demands Hezbollah, August 21, 2006; Europe commits troops, August 26, 2006). Occasional Lebanese, or Hezbollah, perspectives struggled against the "factual" assumptions of the omniscient Western hegemonic voice imbedded in the news and against labeling that undermined their credibility (Will cease-fire endure? August 15, 2006; Bengali, August 16, 2006; Al-Qaida brags, September 12, 2006; Rosenberg, August 20, 2006; U.N. chief tries, August 29, 2006). Texts often enclosed key terms or phrases of Hezbollah perspectives in orphan quotes to signal to readers the questionable accuracy of the statement (Will cease-fire endure? August 15, 2006).

Phase IV: Look Away! The Aftermath, September and October 2006

The withdrawal of news attention from the war in Lebanon effectively eliminated opportunities for challenges to the U.S.-Israeli construction of the summer conflict and submerged unsightly details of their execution of the war. Thus, breaking news of broad international criticism and possible sanctions against Israel's use of cluster bombs during the last days of the war and in the midst of cease-fire negotiations was followed up in *The Seattle Times* only in passing allusions in news summaries months later (Europe commits troops, August 26, 2006; Fadel, September 1, 2006; Mideast Digest, Oct. 21, 2006; Around the Globe, March 21, 2007). In comparison, *The New York Times* ran ten stories based on official records and with few comments from officials about ongoing investigations into Israel's use of cluster bombs. In four substantial news items dealing with the topic between October 2006 and January 2007, for example, *The New York Times* reported that the Bush administration was mired in debate over whether to impose sanctions on Israel over what it described as "only a technical violation" of U.S. and international policies on the use of these weapons that disproportionately harm civilians (Cloud and Myre, January 28, 2007). The same *New York Times* story also reported that the United States had banned sale of cluster weapons to Israel following its earlier war in Lebanon after Congress "found that Israel had used the weapons in civilian areas during its 1982 invasion."

News coverage of the details of the Israel government report on its use of cluster bombs and the terms of the "agreements that govern Israel's use of American cluster munitions" may have been hampered by U.S. government classification of much of the relevant information and the absence of official comment on the investigations (Cloud and Myre, Israel January 28, 2007). However, given the agenda setting function of *The New York Times,* this does not adequately explain why none of the details it published and no mention of the outspoken criticism from the U.N. Mine Action Coordination Center or the Israeli military inquiry into use of cluster bombs in Lebanon ever appeared in *The Seattle Times* (see, e.g., Myre, November 21, 2006). Rather, the omission of this news and the withdrawal of coverage of the war as details of the devastation of Lebanon were emerging suggest the power of U.S.-Western government elites to direct news through their attention and inattention to topics. The silence of elite spokespeople on the war and its aftermath reduced the news hole available for coverage of Lebanon and eliminated significant ongoing issues from the public gaze. Thus, for example, neither the difficult clean up of cluster bombs nor the continuing Israeli-Lebanese border tensions following the cease-fire ever appeared in the *Seattle Times.* The silence effected through withdrawal of Western elite voices further served to eliminate discussion of the war at a time when such coverage might undermine the Western ideology of war as the path to peace.

Conclusions

To explore the peace journalism implications of news shifts that accompany a wave of coverage of a key event, this study examined all of the newspaper content related to the summer 2006 war in Lebanon during the roughly three-month period of news attention to the war. As anticipated (and reflected in the design of this study), the *Seattle Times* published a wave of increased volume, diversity and intensity of news on Lebanon during the period of the war. The nature of the coverage during the wave evidenced four phases, moving from elite domination of the news through more contested and diverse perspectives and back to elite domination before virtually disappearing again from the newspaper. The more detailed discussion of the nature of these coverage phases served to answer the four research questions posed at the outset of this study.

The findings demonstrate that the wave of news coverage of the 2006 war in Lebanon did lead journalists to use a greater diversity of non-elite sources for a time in their reporting. The greatest increase in the diversity of sources, and in the divergence of views and perspectives presented on the war, occurred during the peak of coverage of the war. The findings also provide evidence that the nature of coverage of the nations and peoples involved in the war changed, as a wider range of sources gave voice to a fuller scope of parties to the conflict and provided opportunities for greater depth, richness, and challenge to the rather dualistic and simplistic portrayals that dominated the onset of coverage. The increased range of voices both directly and indirectly challenged the expressed policies and priorities of the U.S.-West, contesting their construction of the war, its causes, its effects, and its objectives. And, it may be said, these shifts did move the coverage of the war—albeit only slightly and very temporarily—toward some peace journalism practices.

How then, is it possible to argue that war journalism dominates the news? Or, put differently, what does it suggest that peace journalism practices raised their heads even briefly during the heated coverage of a hot war? As an exploratory case study, conclusions must be limited to the case at hand and implications for broader peace and war journalism practices are tentative at best. Nonetheless, this analysis of one newspaper's wave of coverage of the 2006 summer war in Lebanon suggests that increased news attention (and the resulting increase in the news hole) during a key event provides an opportunity for the inclusion of multiple voices and perspectives that can move coverage toward greater peace journalism practices. The surge in coverage opened a short and narrow path for narratives that humanized victims on both sides of the conflict, positioned the war within the global political aspirations of the United States, exposed the devastation of both Israel and Lebanon, and provided more complex portraits of all the parties to the conflict.

This wave of coverage, accompanied by an increase in news space and the inclusion of voices of difference and challenge, was transient; its shifts occasional, partial and, to a large degree, ineffectual. Without active commentary, engagement and endorsement from the elite base that so dominates news coverage, voices of difference appeared and disappeared rapidly, receiving scant validation by and through media coverage. When the challenges did not gain support from the dominant elite, they either dissipated through their own diffusion (i.e., in the way that a social movement loses "energy" through the perception that its message has been "heard," see McAdam and Snow, 2007, and see Gamson and Wolfsfeld, 1993), or disappeared when the elite voices upon which the media depend reclaimed their dominance and redirected reporting away from voices of opposition. This redirection (see essay by Peleg and Mandelzis, this volume) effectively silenced criticism, which had limited independent ability to attract the media gaze.

Thus, while this study of news coverage of the Lebanon war documents a brief window of opportunity in which journalists might exercise choices that could reflect greater peace journalism reporting, the structural and on-the-ground conditions of such reporting may not favor altered journalism practices that require both individual initiative and systematic change. While the findings of this study fall far short of sufficient to support such a claim, might it be argued that the inclusion of voices of difference within this surge of war coverage is sufficient primarily to justify media's self-interested claims of balance, fairness and objectivity? Should those seeking to advance peace journalism examine whether the shifts observed in this study function not as a mechanism for advancing but for opposing challenges to the elite and to ingrained media practices? To what degree might further research help highlight the extent to which the observed brief challenges to the dominant discourse support the strategic myth that the media function as a platform for wide-open public debate (eliminating the need for more sweeping changes in journalism practices) rather than afford real and credible opportunities for the expression of alternative views? In a similar vein, it may be useful to consider whether the limited and contained expression of dissonance affords cathartic release for growing anti-elite perspectives that actually helps consolidate the centers of power and maintain the status quo.

Further research is needed to explore the degree to which the aborted inclusion of voices of difference within a news wave might best be understood as the product of strategic silence in which the media and the officials on whom they depend are complicit in marginalizing and then removing challenges to the dominant view. Such a finding would pose new obstacles to the broad adoption of a peace journalism praxis.

Notes

1.   The author gratefully acknowledges financial support for this and ongoing study of the role of media in international conflict from a Canadian Consulate Canadian Studies Research Grant, the Pacific Northwest Canadian Studies Consortium, the Washington State University College of Liberal Arts and its Office of Research, and the Toda Institute for Global Peace and Policy Research. For research contributions, challenging questions, and stimulating discussions during their studies at Washington State University, the author wishes to thank Bruno Baltodano and Jay Hmielowski. All errors of omission and commission are the author's.
2.   A *Lexis-Nexis* search of the entire *Seattle Times* for the term Hezbollah found no stories during the six months prior to the war and mentions only in briefs and digest items from October 2006 through early 2007.

3.   According to annual research reported in *Editor & Publisher* and by the Project
      for Excellence in Journalism (e.g., *The State of the News Media 2006, An Annual
      Report on American Journalism*), newspapers with an average daily circulation
      between 100,000 and 250,000 represented the largest percentage circulation in the
      United States, reaching some 20 percent of total daily newspaper readership. The
      dominance of this mid-sized daily newspaper in the U.S. market has held steady
      for several years.

References

Bennett, W. L. 1990. Toward a theory of press-state relations in the United States. *Journal of Communication*, 40(2), 103-127.

Bennett, W. L. 1996. *News: The politics of illusion*. Longman Publishers.

Brosius, H. B., and Eps, P. 1995. Prototyping through events. *European Journal of Communication*, 10, 391-412.

Cobb, R. W., and Elder, C. D. 1972. *Participation in American politics: The dynamics of agenda building*. Baltimore: Johns Hopkins University Press.

Entman, R. M. 1993. Framing: Toward clarification of a fractured paradigm. *Journal of Communication*, 43(4), 51-58.

Entman, R. M. 2004. *Projections of power: Framing news, public opinion, and U.S. foreign policy*. Chicago: The University of Chicago Press.

Galtung, J. 1998. Peace journalism: What, why, who, how, when, where. Paper presented in the workshop, *"What are journalists for?"* TRANSCEND, Taplow Court, UK, September 3-6.

Gamson, W.A., and Wolfsfeld, G. 1993. Movements and Media as Interacting Systems. *The Annals of the American Academy of Political and Social Science*, 528 (1), 114-125.

Iyengar, S. 1990. Framing responsibility for political issues: The case of poverty. *Political Behavior*, 12(1), 19-40.

Iyengar, S. 1991. *Is anyone responsible? How television frames political issues*. The University of Chicago Press: Chicago and London.

Kempf, W. 2001. News media and conflict escalation – a comparative study of the Gulf War coverage in American and European media. In: S.A. Nohrstedt and R. Ottosen (eds.). *Journalism and the New World Order. Vol. I. Gulf War, National News Discourses and Globalization*. Göteborg: Nordicom.

Kepplinger, H. M. and Daschmann, G. (1997). Today's news – tomorrow's context: A dynamic model of news processing. *Journal of Broadcasting & Electronic Media*, 41(4), 548-565.

Lawrence, R. G. 2001. Define events: Problem definition in the media arena. In R. P. Hart and B. H. Sparrow (eds.), *Politics, discourse, and American society* (pp. 91-110). Lanham, MD: Rowman & Littlefield Publishers, Inc.

Lynch, J., and McGoldrick, A. 2005. *Peace Journalism*. Stroud, UK: Hawthorn Press.

Mandelzis, L. (2003). The changing image of the enemy in the news discourse of Israeli newspapers 1993-1994. *Conflict & Communication Online*, 2(1), 2-12.

McAdam, D., and Snow, D.A. (eds.). 2007. *Social Movements: Readings on Their Emergence, Mobilization, and Dynamics*. New York: Oxford University Press.

Nelson, T. E., Clawson, R. A., and Oxley, Z. M. 1997. Media framing of a civil liberties conflict and its effects on tolerance. *The American Political Science Review*, 91(3), 567-583.

Ross, S. D., and Bantimaroudis, P. 2006. Frame shifts and catastrophic events: The attacks on September 11, 2001, and New York Time's portrayals of Arafat and Sharon. *Mass Communication & Society*, 9(1), 85-101.

Wolfsfeld, G. 2001. Political waves and democratic discourse: Terrorism waves during the Oslo peace process. In W. L. Bennett and R. M. Entman, eds., *Mediated politics: Communication in the future of democracy*. New York: Cambridge University Press.

Wolfsfeld, G., and Sheafer, T. 2006. Competing actors and the construction of political news: The contest over waves in Israel. *Political Communication*, 23, 333-354.

Newspaper Sources

Al-Qaida brags, *Seattle Times*, Sept. 12, 2006.

Allam, Dozens of children killed in Israeli airstrike, *Seattle Times*, July 31, 2006.

Allam, Lebanese struggle to stay with families, *Seattle Times*, July 30, 2006.

Around the Globe, *Seattle Times*, March 21, 2007.

Bazzi, Experts fear the Offensive in Lebanon will inspire, *Seattle Times*, Aug. 2, 2006.

Bengali, Hezbollah's weapons cache, *Seattle Times*, Aug. 16, 2006.

Bengali and Nissenbaum, Israel falls short of its objectives, *Seattle Times*, Aug. 13, 2006.

Bengali and Strobel, U.S., France join in cease-fire call in Lebanon war, *Seattle Times*, Aug. 6, 2006.

Browne Jr., J.H., Northwest Voices: The malignant rumor, *Seattle Times*, July 30, 2006.

Cloud and Myre, Israel may have violated arms pact, New York Times, Jan. 28, 2007.

Diamond, T., Northwest Voices: The tree of liberty, *Seattle Times*, July 23, 2006.

Dunn, A., Northwest Voices: Unwinning strategy, *Seattle Times*, July 22, 2006.

Europe commits troops, *Seattle Times*, Aug. 26, 2006.

Extract, B., Northwest Voices: Chastened survivors, *Seattle Times*, Aug. 6, 2006.

The Eye-catchers, *Seattle Times*, July 16, 2006.

Fadel, Anger converts victims' families to Hezbollah, Aug. 7, 2006.

Fadel, Cluster bombs, *Seattle Times*, Sept. 1, 2006.

Fadel, War fuels anti-American sentiment, *Seattle Times*, Aug. 11, 2006.

Fryer, Cantwell, McGavick agree on some Lebanon issues, *Seattle Times*, July 28, 2006.

Gaza and Lebanon, An endless summer, *Seattle Times*, July 16, 2006.

Give a green light for full negotiations, *Seattle Times*, July 20, 2006.

Goodstein, Andrew, Northwest Voices: Again, never again, *Seattle Times*, Aug. 1, 2006.

Hanson, D., Northwest Voices: Survival in imbalance, *Seattle Times*, Aug. 7, 2006.

Harkavy, R., Northwest Voices: Embers of Terror, *Seattle Times*, July 23, 2006.

Hawkins, Mike, Northwest Voices: Delirium sets in, *Seattle Times*, July 30, 2006.

Hsu and King, Violence in Mideast hitting close to home, *Seattle Times*, July 18, 2006.

Hulays, Z., Northwest Voices: The beleaguered side, *Seattle Times*, July 19, 2006.

Israel replaces commander, *Seattle Times*, Aug. 9, 2006.

Jeffers, U.S. lacks moral authority, *Seattle Times*, Aug. 9, 2006.

Long, A glimmer of hope after weeks of war, *Seattle Times*, Aug. 6, 2006.

Losses leaving Israelis skeptical, *Seattle Times*, July 27, 2006.

Marsh, N., Northwest Voices: No match, *Seattle Times*, July 23, 2006.

Mideast Digest, *Seattle Times*, Oct. 21, 2006.

Mideast fighting signals widening conflict, *Seattle Times*, July 14, 2006.

Mullin, War in homeland unites local Lebanese Americans, *Seattle Times*, Aug. 10, 2006.

Myre, Israel orders investigation of bomb use in Lebanon, New York Times, Nov. 21, 2006.

Nissenbaum, Civilian toll puts focus on Israel's response, *Seattle Times*, Aug. 3, 2006.

Nissenbaum, Can talking halt killing in Middle East? *Seattle Times*, July 18, 2006.

Nissenbaum, Civilian toll puts focus on Israel's response, *Seattle Times*, Aug. 3, 2006.

Nissenbaum, Israeli tanks push north, *Seattle Times*, July 23, 2006.

Nissenbaum, Rocket attack 'like nothing you can imagine,' *Seattle Times*, Aug. 7, 2006.

Nissenbaum and Strobel, Israel, Lebanon support peace plan, *Seattle Times*, Aug. 12, 2006.

Nissenbaum and Strobel, Prospect of ground war weighs on Mideast, *Seattle Times*, July 22, 2006.

Osawa, S., Northwest Voices: Where's the fire, *Seattle Times*, July 23, 2006.

Postman, Let's face it, it's WWIII, *Seattle Times*, July 16, 2006.

Rahman, J., Northwest Voices: God takes no hand, The *Seattle Times*, July 31, 2006.

Rosenberg, With Iran's help, *Seattle Times*, Aug. 20, 2006.

Rosenberg and Fadel, All-out war, then Monday cease-fire? *Seattle Times*, Aug. 13, 2006.

Strobel and Landay, U.S. forces still struggle, *Seattle Times*, Sept. 11, 2006.

Tu, Demonstrators call for peace, *Seattle Times*, Aug. 12, 2006.

War Journalism as Media Manipulation: Seesawing between the Second Lebanon War and the Iranian Nuclear Threat

Lea Mandelzis and Samuel Peleg

Introduction: War Journalism and the Art of Diversion

Conventional coverage of conflicts is constantly and consistently marred by overly dramatic and sensational reporting due to structural, economic and professional traits of journalism. Since the early 1970s, a different orientation of conflict narration has emerged mainly, but not exclusively, out of communication studies to challenge the traditional militant approach. This new school of thought has come to be known, for a lack of a better term, as "peace journalism" (Hackett and Zhao, 2005; Lynch and Mc-Goldrick, 2005; Shinar and Kempf, 2007). The two schools are divided on various issues regarding the most appropriate manner to describe conflicts in the written and electronic media. Briefly put, the conventional coverage promotes a narrow perspective of dyadic relationships and simplistic dichotomies of "good against evil," "moral versus immoral" and "righteous" as opposed to "unjust." Such reporting is focused on events and symptoms rather than on reasons, circumstances and consequences. As such, the traditional reporting of conflicts avoids contextualization, which might put a damper on the excitement of the moment. Peace journalism, on the other hand, adheres to coverage in which the historical, cultural, political and economic background is underscored, sequences of occurrences and developments are observed, and ethical and moral implications of conflicts are analyzed and stressed (Galtung, 2000; Lynch and McGoldrick, 2005). Owing to its belligerent and confrontational character, of presenting conflicts in an assumingly attractive way, conventional journalism has earned the synonym of "war journalism."

79

In many instances, war journalism relies on manipulation to preserve its advantage as a supplier of stimuli and thrill. Such a modus operandi emerges at the junction where expectations of political leaders and journalists converge (Peleg, 2002). For the former, alarming portrayal of enemies, threats or dangers is valuable to introduce their leadership skills and to expedite group cohesion processes; for the latter the quest for drama is the name of the game and it must be maintained in light of competition and struggle for audience attention among competing news channels. If drama does not exist "on the ground," then drama must be sought, created or discovered elsewhere or anywhere for that matter.

The theoretical framework of our discussion is therefore the recently growing domain of media manipulation. We focus on a case of displacing the attention of readers and watchers from one arena to another (Mandelzis, 2003) and replacing divisive feelings such as dismay, defiance and depression with unifying emotions such as anxiety and uncertainty. Through such displacements, reporters stretch the meaning of the term security (and insecurity) to new dimensions. In our specific exploration, we follow closely the gradual and ongoing diversion process in the Israeli written media reports from the unfolding debacle of the Second Lebanon War (July-August, 2006) to the intoxicating but unifying stimulant of the Iranian nuclear threat. In highly evasive journalistic coverage, the center of attention began gradually but steadily to shift from military stalemates and battle casualties to emerging worldwide threats and admonitions from Teheran. This article is a preliminary discussion of the process of diversion from one topic to the other, from one geographical arena to another and from one manipulated atmosphere, which eventually disserved and destabilized the status quo, to one that promoted cohesion and unity.

The Wonders of Media Manipulation

Media manipulation is a very powerful tool in the hands of interested players who aim to change the socioeconomic priority-scale, reset the political agenda and invoke broad-based popular legitimacy to support their goals. Media manipulation relies heavily on various propaganda techniques, selective information, suppression of certain viewpoints, and the ever-popular diversion of public attention. These diverse methods are based on a common assumption that the general public has a limited attention span and a short memory. Distraction can be applied to individuals as well as to entire nations. For example, the *ad hominem* (Latin for "against the man") mechanism is an old-age trick to discredit a person rather than a claim or an opinion. Instead of addressing the substance of an argument or producing evidence against a specific claim, an *ad hominem* response attacks or appeals to a characteristic or belief of the individual making the argument or claim. This tactic is often translated to and practiced in collective discourses, chiefly by appealing to nationalism and similar group-cohesion systems such as local patriotism, camaraderie or class solidarity.

Here, opposing views are tarnished by appealing to nationalistic sentiments and group pride. These sentiments are invoked by honing the contrast between "us" and "them," either by emphasizing superiority over the Other in various ways, or by eliciting fear or dislike of the antagonist. Such feelings are stimulated by inaccurate generalizations, half-truths, labeling, stigmatization, and stereotyping. The following comment of a senior State Department official, who was quoted in a *New York Times* article, is a perfect example: "You want to know what I really think of the Europeans? I think they have been wrong on just about every major international issue for the past 20 years" (Ash, Anti-Europeanism in America, NYT, February 13, 2003).

There are other ploys of media manipulation and they include marginalization, demonization, word laundering, misrepresentation of opinions, and scapegoating. Marginalization is a prevalent and devious form of media manipulation; it deliberately focuses only on mainstream "formal" sources of information and ignores information, arguments and objections that arrive from alternative sources. Non-elite ideas are blatantly eschewed as "fringe" and irrelevant, and their proponents are disparaged or accused of having a self-interested agenda. This sense of marginalization is aptly expressed by the anti-Iraqi war activist Warren Langley in a *San Francisco Chronicle* interview:

"I think there are a lot of people out there who feel the way I do, but haven't wanted to come forward because they're afraid of being identified with a fringe group…" Langley said. "I don't believe in all the things that all the (anti-war) groups stand for, but we all do share one thing in common: I do believe that this war is wrong" (Garofoli, March 4, 2003).

Demonization of the other is one of the most ancient tools in conflict. In order to win over the dispute by unifying one's side behind the cause, the most efficient and rapid vehicle is to vilify and denigrate the adversary. The more evil, scary, and menacing the image of the rival, the greater the resolve and commitment attained. Calls to nationalism work like this in many instances; disagreeable views are ascribed to an out-group or hated group, and thus dismissed out of hand. This approach, carried to extremes, in the hands of U.S. Senator Joseph McCarthy became a form of suppression, where anyone disapproving of the government was considered "un-American" and "Communist" and was likely to be condemned. Equally distorting and alarming is labeling all those opposed to neoconservative policies as "left-wingers," thus evoking existing prejudices against Communism to de-legitimize opponents.

Word laundering can be highly effective when skillfully employed. Distraction by semantics involves using euphemistically pleasing terms to obscure the truth. For example, saying "choice" or "reproductive rights" instead of the accurate term "abortion," or "pro-life" instead of "anti-abortion." Another memorable example was frequently used in the antebellum American South when people commonly referred to "states rights" instead of "slavery." This Orwellian approach to language is reminiscent of Humpty Dumpty's rebuttal of Alice's protest:

> "When *I* use a word," Humpty Dumpty said, in a rather scornful tone, "it means just what I choose it to mean, neither more nor less."

> "The question is," said Alice, "whether you *can* make words mean so many different things."

> "The question is," said Humpty Dumpty, "which is to be master—that's all" (Carroll, *Through the Looking Glass*, 1871).

Misrepresenting the intentions or expressions of another side is also a very common tactic in media manipulation. In philosophy it is known as the "straw man fallacy," which is the lumping together of a strong opposition argument and one or many weak ones to create a simplistic unconvincing argument that can easily be refuted. Such was the case in the public debate surrounding the 2003 invasion of Iraq when all arguments against that policy were grouped together under the umbrella of "pacifism," and thus were more easily exposed to refutation by arguments for war in general. As with most persuasion methods, it can easily be applied in reverse, in this case, to group all those who supported the invasion together and label them as "warmongers."

Finally, scapegoating is basically the diversion of attention from one phenomenon to another, or from one unfavorable sequence of events to a seemingly more interesting and captivating development to dwarf or nullify the initial incident. Distraction by scapegoat has been useful to numerous leaders in the course of history who employed it as an evasion from internal difficulties to external adventures, or as a pressure release valve to dodge responsibility or elude consequences. Barry Levinson's 1997 film *Wag the Dog* is a brilliant example of how scapegoating works: In order to divert public attention from a fornicating president, a shrewd advisor concocts a fabricated war and sways the media to create a spin around it. Naturally, hype of the new conflict pushes the president's moral transgression into oblivion. But scapegoating is slippery; it must distract the public for long periods of time from an important issue by one that occupies more news time. When the strategy works, you have a war or other media event taking attention away from misbehaving or crooked leaders. When the strategy does not work, the leader's misbehavior remains in the press, and the war is derided as an attempted distraction.

Chronologies of War and Nuclear Threat

The following heuristic exploration brings forth such an attempt at diversion by the Israeli media during and after the Second Lebanon War in the summer of 2006. We attempt to expose a linkage between war coverage from Lebanon and emanating reports about the Iranian nuclear threat. Our contention is that the less invigorating and successful the war became, the more menacing and disturbing the Iranian story grew. "Linkage politics" is a political science term that connotes the strategic association between two policies or two political agendas, usually between internal and external politics, in order to shift attention from one to the other. Leaders in trouble create a correlation between two priorities where they can effortlessly alternate from a faltered undertaking to a relatively more successful or sympathetic endeavor. Next we introduce the topics of coverage—the war in Lebanon, the Iranian threat and the linkage formed between them.

Period I: The Lebanon War from Determination to Frustration

Our task is to demonstrate the linkage between two major news items that gained journalistic attention in the summer of 2006. We argue that the pattern of their media occurrence would be inversely related: while descriptions of the war in Lebanon were becoming less and less optimistic and enthusiastic, the tone of the Iranian threat reports grew more and more menacing and provoking. To contrast the two cases, we chose to follow the Institute for National Security Studies' *INSS Report on the Second Lebanon War: Strategic Dimensions* and the book *Captives in Lebanon* (2007) by two prominent reporters, Ofer Shelach of Israeli TV Channel 10 and Yoav Limor of Channel 1 News. Their chronological accounts of the war will be juxtaposed with the daily appearances of the Iranian threat as reported in the daily *Ha'aretz* newspaper. The discussion identifies two periods: (1) the war itself, from July 12 to August 14; and (2) the 30-day period of the war's aftermath tremors and the growing coverage of the Iranian threat intended to divert attention from the internal unrest to greener pastures of consensus and shared anxiety.

The following summary reflects the "narrative of the war" proffered by Israeli media in which they generally adopted "war journalism" strategies, such as failure to report casualties on the "other" side. Such practices were bolstered by evasion of military failures through increased attention to the Iranian story.

The war broke out on July 12 after a Hezbollah unit ambushed an Israeli army patrol car, killing three soldiers and kidnapping two others. In pursuit of the fleeing commandos, an Israeli tank set off an explosive detonation and its crew of five perished. The Israeli government approved a "limited" operation against Hezbollah forces spread along the Lebanese-Israeli border. All day long artillery fire restricted to the border areas was exchanged between the two sides. The next morning, July 13, Israel launched the "Apt Retaliation" operation (later it was renamed "Redirection") in which the Israeli air force attacked more than 80 targets in Lebanon, including Hezbollah headquarters and military camps. One major target was the runways of Beirut's international airport. Hezbollah retaliated by launching 197 rockets toward northern Israel, reaching as far as Haifa and killing two civilians and injuring dozens. The same day, the reporting linkage between the tenacity of Hezbollah and the encouragement of Iran debuts in the Israeli press. The third day, July 14, witnessed 182 more missiles from Lebanon to Israeli towns and villages, causing damages and killing two elderly civilians. The Israeli air force increased its bombing on southern Lebanon, while the Israeli navy blockaded Lebanese ports. An Israeli missile ship was hit by a Hezbollah rocket and four of its crew were killed. By nightfall, it was reported that President Mahmoud Ahmadinejad had announced from Teheran that, in light of Israeli aggression, Iran would not cooperate with the G-8 countries' request that it halt its nuclear plans.

On July 15, Israeli air raids reached northern Lebanon, including the Shiite town of Baal Beck. Hassan Nassaralla, the Hezbollah leader, declared that his warriors would surprise Israel. That day, 187 rockets hit Israel and reached as far as Tiberius. Alongside reports on the war, the G-8 summit in Edinburgh received coverage from Israeli journalists, with particular emphasis on statements by American representatives to the meeting about the tie between Iran, North Korea, Syria, and Hezbollah. A further escalation marked the fifth day of the war, July 16, when a direct hit in the Haifa main train station killed eight workers. Across the border, the IDF (Israeli Defense Force) attacked Beirut and Tyr, while the Israeli Civil Defense Authority issued a missile warning that extended all the way south to Tel Aviv. The editorial in *Ha'aretz* that day was titled "Iran bears a direct involvement," implicating Iran with incitement. The association between Hezbollah and Iran was further enhanced the next day when a barrage of rockets hit Haifa again inflicting destruction in mainly poor neighborhoods. Zeev Sheiff, a leading commentator, wrote that "the apex is still to come and it hinges upon Iran's decision to arm Hezbollah with longer range missiles" (*Ha'aretz*, July 17, 2006, p. 1).

Meanwhile on the ground, the war escalated further when Israeli Defense Minister Amir Peretz authorized mobilization of reserve forces. Israeli Prime Minister Ehud Olmert addressed the Knesset with a militant speech and received standing ovations. By the sixth day, Israeli public opinion was fully supportive of the military operation, and the two political novices Olmert and Peretz rose to their highest popularity owing to their resolve on the war. At this juncture, any internal rifts were latent and the need to bring forth other issues in journalistic coverage was less acute. However, by now, the first stage of the war, which was persistently termed an "operation" by the Israeli officials, was waning. The second stage was about to begin, or as Shelach and Limor wrote, events were undergoing a transition from the opening chapter: "This is not a War" to the subsequent one: "Grey Time," marking the shift from the initial exhilaration of warfare to the banality of the battlefield.

Israeli eagerness and enthusiasm for the war began to falter in the third week. Gradually, discouraging news infiltrated the Israeli public discourse. The troops were bogged down in battles against paramilitary guerrillas they were supposed to vanquish easily. The growing number of casualties was alarming. Small Lebanese villages such as Binth Jbail and Marun-a-Rass turned into bloody battlefields where 25 Israeli soldiers were killed and 50 injured. Some of them fell victim to "friendly fire." In addition, when four U.N. observers were killed in an Israeli bombing, Secretary General Kofi Anan saw it as a deliberate attack. Prime Minister Olmert apologized in a gesture that could not have helped improve the deteriorating image of the war in the eyes of Israelis. Initial protests were set in motion, and journalistic reports started to lose their fervor.

Steadily, and in tandem with the wavering descriptions of the war, Iran came back into the journalistic coverage. On July 29, Ahmadinejad called for a cease-fire and threatened "dire consequences" if Israel declined.

By that date, Shelach and Limor identified a third stage in their analysis, which they call "cognition molding": the inculcation of a framed reality in the Israeli collective conscience to justify the military action against Hezbollah. Such a policy became urgent in light of emerging Israeli frustration and mounting impressions of military failure. *Newsweek* correspondent Christopher Dickey summed up this mood succinctly when he wrote: "the bottom line is that Hezbollah is winning the battle" ("Let It Bleed," *Newsweek*, July 27, 2006).

July 30 further aggravated the withdrawal of public support when another Israeli air raid killed 28 civilians in the Lebanese village of Kana. The incident triggered a wave of condemnations against Israel, and U.S. Secretary of State Condoleezza Rice's visit to Beirut was cancelled. The next day, Israel suspended all military air activities over Lebanon for 48 hours to investigate the massacre. Iran used the Kana incident to remind the world that Israel understands only force, a frame widely covered in the Israeli press. August brought more Israeli escalation with attacks on Beirut itself, and Hezbollah's Nasarallah promised to retaliate with missiles to Tel Aviv. The Iranian president declared, at a summit of Muslim states in Malaysia, that "the Israeli presence in the Middle East is an American ploy and that Israel's aggression in Lebanon might trigger a new wave of global terrorism" (*Ha'aretz* August 5, 2006, p. 1). The next four days reported new peaks of hostilities as the two sides vied for achievements before international efforts for cease-fire materialized. On August 11, 24 Israeli soldiers were dead and 85 wounded. Iran threatened to send troops to reinforce Hezbollah, but the next day, August 12, exactly one month from the beginning of the war, the U.N. Security Council adopted Resolution 1701 for a cease-fire in Lebanon. The next day, August 13, the Israeli government and Hezbollah agreed to the U.N. decision, and on the August 14, at 8 a.m., a cease-fire was declared and the official war was over.

That same day, an Israeli public opinion poll revealed the grim mood of anger and frustration that was gripping Israeli society: 52% believed that the IDF was unsuccessful in the war; 62% gave Prime Minister Olmert a bad grade in handling the war; and 65% gave a similar mark to Defense Minister Peretz. During the last days of the war, two leading Israeli columnists—Shavit (*Ha'aretz,* August 11, 2006, p. 1) and Barnea (*Yediot Acharonot*, August 10, 2006, pp. 1, 18) were very critical of Olmert in essays titled "Olmert Has to Go" and "Olmert—Get Up and Leave," respectively. As prominent shapers of public opinion, the two columnists both set and reflected the atmosphere of the aftermath of the war.

Period II: The Aftermath of the War and the Rise of the Iranian Threat

Within days of the war's end, the first of the Israeli protest campsites was erected. Calls for an inquiry committee to investigate the political decision-making processes as well as the army's military strategy during the war were heard all over Israel. Upon the reserve forces' return home, the protest gained momentum and thousands joined vigil marches and demonstrations. The media sided with the protestors and added their voice to the outcry through editorials and commentary in favor of a major internal inspection. The thought that the mighty Israeli army was incapable of decisively winning over the pseudo-military force of Hezbollah was unbearable to most Israelis. Additionally, the psychological damage to the invincibility of the nation following the barrage of missiles on unprotected civilians was considerable. The sense of relative security Israelis enjoyed for a long period of time was severely impaired.

In the very first day of the cease-fire, three ominous articles appear in the first two pages of *Ha'aretz*: widely esteemed, veteran columnist Zeev Sheiff led the way with an essay called "Indecisively and belatedly" (*Ha'aretz*, August 13, 2006, p. 1) and, "Who really won? If we won, this is not a good enough victory" (*Ha'aretz*, August 15, 2006, p. 1). On the same page, Aluf Ben issued his own *J'accuse!* with an article called "20 Questions to Investigate." These headlines built up pressure as the snowball of opposition continued to roll, and a chain of military senior officers resigned shortly after, including the IDF chief of staff, Dan Halutz.

The menacing schism between the authorities and the population activated the journalistic escape mechanism. Suddenly, the Iranian threat loomed brighter and the statements from Teheran wrestled with the fomenting internal turbulence for media attention. Steadily, as the public unrest widened, the nuclear menace became more and more newsworthy, with Iranian President Ahmadinejad taking media center stage. On August 16, as the public debate about the war became more and more visible in Israel, the newspaper headlines placed the Iranian president in a "victory speech" in front of thousands of supporters in the northern Iranian city of Ardabil stating that "we must settle the scores with America and Israel once and for all" (*Ha'aretz*, 16/8/2006, p. 1). Another headline for the day read, "Olmert: We will have to check ourselves on all levels" (Ibid.). Two days after the end of the war, the two topics were contending for media primacy, but that was about to change.

The Lebanon War and the Iranian threat were wedded by the "best man" Syria. On August 17, the *Ha'aretz* editorial titled "The No-Partner in Damascus" reiterated the affinity between Syria, Iran, and Hezbollah. The article preceded an official visit of the Syrian army chief of staff to Iran to observe military maneuvers by the Iranian army. The apex of the visit was a strategic cooperation pact signed between the two army commanders. At the ceremony, the host chief of staff, Iranian General Ata Alla Salhi, boasted that "his army is ready for any Israeli aggression" and that "the enemy was bewildered and surprised from Hezbollah's courage." Iran, he added, sees Syria's security as its own (*Ha'aretz*, August 20, 2006, p. 1). Shmuel Rozner, U.S. correspondent to *Ha'aretz,* further linked the Lebanon war with the Iranian threat by reporting that same day that "the war improved chances for U.N. sanctions on Iran" (*Ha'aretz,* August 12, 2006, p. 1). Still on the same day, but on an internal page, Hasson informed *Ha'aretz* readers (August 20, 2006, p. 1) that "the reserve soldiers' protest is gaining momentum."

The timing of the militant Iranian-Syrian declarations and the well publicized strategic agreement between the two allies was carefully chosen: Iran promised to respond to the U.N. Security Council's July 31 ultimatum by August 22, a week prior to its expiration on August 31. Hence, this was a show of force to demonstrate Iran's military capacity in case anyone decided to attack her. A day before the deadline, *Ha'aretz* showed a scary color photo of an Iranian long-range missile launch on page two, a very rare editorial decision. Numerous speculations as to the Iranian reply filled the press, with a clear tendency toward the bleak and pessimistic. The next day headlines were overt: "Iran Notified the U.N.: We Will Continue to Enrich Uranium" (Melman, *Ha'aretz,* August 13, 2006 p. 1). The small print subtitle, which read "Iran declared it wants nuclear energy for peaceful purposes," was eclipsed by the hullabaloo of the main item. Melman, *Ha'aretz* correspondent for intelligence affairs, elaborated on a secret American report: "Within Five Years, Iran will Produce a Nuclear Bomb" (*Ha'aretz,* August 24, 2006, p. 1). He reported that Iran already had chemical and biological weapons and the largest stockpile of ballistic missiles in the Middle East. The tendency to overshadow increasing internal Israeli dispute with the Iranian danger persisted until the end of the month. It was further bolstered and justified by the approaching expiration day of the U.N. ultimatum to Iran.

The same pattern appeared on August 25. A report on the protest movement by the Jerusalem correspondent Galilee called "The Israeli Bermuda Triangle" was obscured by a top-of-the-page account: "Air

Force Commander will be in Charge of the Iranian Front." In the details, the report disclosed that "Israel speeds up its preparations of a possible confrontation with Iran" (*Ha'aretz*, August 25, 2006, p. 1). Again on August 27, when Prime Minister Olmert pondered a possible inquiry committee with his cabinet to the chants of protestors outside his window, and Sheiff continued his dissection of the war under the heading "Logistical Failure that Brought a Confidence Crisis," the lead headline belonged to Shlomo Shamir's report from Washington: "The U.S. Considers Sanctions on Iran Independently of UN Decisions." Clarification in the text is unambiguous: due to U.N. hesitancy, the American administration would act promptly and swiftly if necessary to suppress the Iranian danger. The next day, August 28, the Associated Press (AP) reported that "Iran has for the first time successfully launched a missile from a submarine." The text pointed out that this particular missile was incapable of carrying a nuclear head, but the story's impact was achieved and increased by the accompanying picture of the portentous *Thaqeb* missile. Another prominent story reported that Iranian President Ahmadinejad had formally opened a heavy water plant that could be used in the production of nuclear weapons.

The U.N. ultimatum to Iran expired on August 31, and the lack of response from Teheran primed the news for the next two days. The tension climbed to unprecedented heights when every penholder surmised everybody's next move. The leading story in *Ha'aretz* came from U.S. correspondent Rozner: "The Ultimatum terminated: the U.S. Pushes for Sanctions." The report was accompanied by a large photo of the nuclear plant in Bushehr. September 1 was also inundated with the same narrative. Melman and Shamir led with a report on "Evidence to Uranium Enrichment by Iran" with an accompanying AP photo showing Ahmadinejad speaking to a huge rally in Teheran. Sheiff followed with a strong recommendation that "a strategic revolution is required and that the Iranian threat must be made the primary military front" (*Ha'aretz*, September 9, 2006, p. 1). The prominence of the Iranian story distracted from a Nir Hasson report about a group of IDF major generals who participated in the war; they now called for "personal conclusions."

On September 11 a formal decision to establish an inquiry committee to investigate Israeli decision-making during the war was announced. Until that day, the Iranian threat reigned supreme and set new records of alarm in articles such as "A State in Danger of Extinction" (Sheleg, *Ha'aretz*, September 3, 2006, p. B-1), where the text began with the following line: "It is hard to believe, but 60 years after the Holocaust, the Jewish people are again in the peril of extermination." Progressively, though, reports on the aftermath of the war recaptured space, eclipsing the Iranian threat story as public discontent became more and more dominant. Tony Blair was interviewed by *Ha'aretz* Editor David Landau and senior correspondent Aluf Ben, generating the following caption: "History will Judge us if we Ignore the Iranian Threat."

Toward a Research Design

This preliminary exploration of the association conventional journalism creates between two seemingly unrelated stories concentrates mainly on the chronological narratives of the Second Lebanon War and the Iranian nuclear threat to indicate how their paired coverage in a leading Israeli newspaper vacillated in accordance with establishment needs and interests. The chronology uncovered an interesting pattern; the two topics studied—the Second Lebanon War and the Iranian threat—vied for ascendancy in news coverage by alternating in and out of news primacy in an orderly fashion. For the first couple of weeks of the war, reports from Lebanon ruled supreme. When, from the Israeli vantage point, the war began to falter, reports of Iran began to appear. The Iranian threat gained more and more space as news from Lebanon soured. In the aftermath of the war and growing internal dissent in Israel, the Iranian threat pushed the Lebanon war out of the headlines completely. A month after the cease-fire agreement of August 14, the two topics regained parity when the Israelis decided to form an inquiry committee into the military operations.

Another intriguing development was the role and image of Iran. In the first stage during the war, Iran was mainly mentioned as a supporter and inspiration for Hezbollah. Occasionally Iranian threats were cited with regard to arms shipments to Lebanon or claims of Israeli aggression. The nuclear issue was underlined only when Iran tied its reluctance to refrain from developing its nuclear capacity with the Israeli aggression in Lebanon. The coverage of the Iranian nuclear threat was augmented immensely following the termination of the war and in striking contrast to declining coverage of the widening rift within Israeli society. While Iran was, at times, a news topic during the war, the content of the stories during the war was strikingly different from the later coverage.

We contend that this juggling of news coverage was a calculated media manipulation to strategically divert popular attention from dissent and remonstration to consensus building and group cohesion. Positioning an existential threat to the State of Israel at the forefront was not a difficult task for politicians because it meshes well with how journalists operate for two primary reasons: The first is linked to the character of news consumers and the way news-gatherers perceive their audience. In an era of "bottom line" journalism and growing competition from new media, media professionals' decision-making has become more market driven. Journalists increasingly seek to create news copy that will suit and appeal to their audience. Their editorial decisions (including elements of news value such as the "un-ambiguity" of the topic (easy to write, easy to digest) vs. complex issues; negative news (bad news sells) vs. positive news; people-related topics (human interest) vs. institution-related stories; focus on elite countries vs. "unimportant" non-elite countries; focus on elite people (movers and shakers vs. "unimportant" people, and so forth) hinge largely on assumptions reporters hold regarding consumer tastes (Galtung and Ruge, 1965). The issue of Iran's nuclear armament is in keeping with these news value indexes; Israeli journalists had no problem giving the "Iranian threat" prominence: It sells papers. The second reason is linked to Lance Bennett's observations that key media professionals—from editors to reporters in the field—tend to gravitate toward middle-of-the-road opinions on any given issue. When conflicts or lack of unanimity arises among elites, lack of consensus will impact and broaden the spectrum of opinion expressed in the news (1990).

References

Ash, T. G. 2003a. "Anti-Europeanism in America." *Hoover Digest Research and Opinion on Public Policy.* No. 2, 2003. http://www.hoover.org/publications/digest/3058211.html.

Bennett, L. 1990. "Toward a Theory of Press-State Relations in the United States." *Journal of Communication*, 40, p. 106.

Carroll, L. 1872. *Through the Looking Glass.* New York: Books of Wonder.

Dickey, C. "Let it Bleed." *Newsweek.* July 26, 2006.

Galtung, J. 2000. "The Task of Peace Journalism." *Ethical Perspectives* 7:2-3, pp. 162-167.

Galtung, J., and Ruge M. 1965. "The structure of foreign news." *Journal of Peace Research*, 2, pp. 64-90.

Garofoli, J. 2003. "In Debt to Our Eyeballs." *San Francisco Chronicle.* March 4, 2003.

Hacket, R. and Zhao, Y. (eds) (2005). *Democratizing Global Media: One World, Many Struggles.* Toronto: Garamond Press.

Lynch, J., and McGoldrick, A. 2005. *Peace Journalism.* Stroud, U.K.: Hawthorn Press.

Mandelzis, L., 2003. "The Changing Image of the Enemy in the Israeli News Discourse." *Conflict & Communication Online*, 2(1). http://www.cco.regener-online.de.

National Security Studies- INSS report on *The Second Lebanon War: Strategic Dimensions* (2007). www.inss.org.il/publications.php?cat=25&incat=&read=247.

Peleg S. 2002. *Zealotry and Vengeance: Quest of a Religious Identity Group.* Lanham: Lexington Books.

Shelah, O., and Limor, Y. 2007. *Captives in Lebanon.* Tel Aviv: Miskal—Yedioth Ahronoth Books and Chemed Books.

Shinar, D., and Kempf, W. (eds) 2007. *Peace Journalism: The State of the Art*. Berlin: Regener.

Newspaper Sources

Aluf, B. "Failures: 20 Questions to Investigate." *Ha'aretz*, August 15, 2006, p. 1.

AP Report. "Iran has for the first time successfully launched a missile from a submarine." Ha'aretz, August 27, 2006. p. 1.

Barnea, N. "Olmert—Get Up and Leave." *Yedioth Acharonot*, August 10, 2006. pp. 1, 18.

Editorial. "The No- Partner in Damascus." *Ha'aretz*, August 17, 2006. Part B-1.

Editorial. "Iran bears a direct involvement." *Ha'aretz*, July 16, 2006. Part B-1.

Galilee, L. "The Israeli Bermuda Triangle." *Ha'aretz*, August 25, 2006. p. 1.

Hasson, N. "The reserve soldiers' protest is gaining momentum." *Ha'aretz,* August 20, 2006. p. 5.

Landau, D. & Aluf, B. "History will Judge us if we Ignore the Iranian Threat." *Ha'aretz*, September 11, 2006. p. 1.

Melman, Y. and Shamir, S. "Evidence to Uranium Enrichment by Iran." *Ha'aretz*, September 1, 2006. p. 1.

Melman, Y. and Shamir, S. "Iran Notified the U.N.: We Will Continue to Enrich Uranium." *Ha'aretz*, August 23, 2006. p. 1.

Melman, Y. "Within Five Years, Iran will Produce a Nuclear Bomb." *Ha'aretz*. August 24, 2006. p. 1.

Rozner, S. "The Ultimatum terminated: the U.S. Pushes for Sanctions." *Ha'aretz*, August 31, 2006. p. 1.

Rozner. S. "The war improved chances for U.N. sanctions on Iran." *Ha'aretz*, August 20, 2006. p. 1.

Shamir, S. "The U.S. Considers Sanctions on Iran Independently of UN Decisions." *Ha'aretz*, August 27, 2006. p. 1.

Shavit, A. "Olmert Has to Go." *Ha'aretz*, August 11, 2006. pp. 1, 16.

Sheiff, Z. "Logistical Failure that Brought a Confidence Crisis." *Ha'aretz*, August 27, 2006. p. 1.

Sheiff, Z. "A strategic revolution is required and that the Iranian threat must be made the primary military front." *Ha'aretz,* September 1, 2006. p. 1.

Sheiff, Z. "Inadequate Winning: Who really won?" *Ha'aretz*, August 15, 2006. p. 1.

Sheiff, Z. "Indecisively and belatedly." *Ha'aretz*, August 13, 2006. p. 1.

Sheiff, Z. "The apex is still to come and it hinges upon Iran's decision to arm Hezbollah with longer range missiles." *Ha'aretz,* July 17, 2006. Part B-1.

Sheleg, Y. "A State in Danger of Extinction." *Ha'aretz*, September 3, 2006. p. B-1.

Video Games as War Propaganda: Can Peace Journalism Offer an Alternative Approach?

Rune Ottosen

The Peace Journalism Approach

Peace journalism, as suggested by Johan Galtung, defines war as a problem in itself and promotes non-violence as a means of conflict resolution (Galtung, 1990, 2002). Galtung's model builds on the dichotomy between what he calls "war journalism" and a "peace journalism" approach. The model includes four main points in which he contrasts the two approaches: war journalism is violence-oriented, propaganda-oriented, elite-oriented and victory-oriented. This approach is often linked to a zero-sum game where the winner (as in sports journalism) takes all. It is a prototype of what one might call traditional mainstream war coverage in which journalists fail to reflect the fact that the media themselves play a role in the conflict, often escalating conflicts by reproducing propaganda developed as part of the participants' media strategies and public relations and publicity campaigns (based on Ottosen, 2007).

The peace journalism approach assumes a moral and ethical point of departure, acknowledging that the media themselves play a role in the propaganda war, intentionally or unintentionally. The peace journalism approach consciously chooses to identify additional options for the readers and viewers by offering a solution-oriented, people-oriented and truth-oriented approach. This includes focusing on possibilities for peace that the conflicting parties might have an interest in hiding. Peace journalism is people-oriented in the sense that it focuses on the victims (often civilian casualties) and thus gives a voice to the voiceless. It is also truth-oriented in the sense that it reveals untruth on all sides and focuses on propaganda as a device for continuing the war (Galtung, 2002). In their book *Peace Journalism* (2005), Jake Lynch and Annabel McGoldrick have further developed

Galtung's model and turned it into a practical tool for journalists. In summary, their ambition is to raise "awareness of non-violence and creativity into the practical job of everyday editing and reporting" (Ibid.). The question explored in this article is whether this experience can be transferred from the realm of news to more entertainment-oriented media.

Computer Games as Mass Media

In his book *Trigger Happy*, Steven Poole argues that computer games must be analyzed within the context of mass media (2004). It is impossible to understand mass culture among youth and ignore the growing computer game industry. By 1999, Americans had named computer games three years in a row as their favorite home entertainment. Twice as many people preferred video games to watching television (Poole, 2004). Three times as many preferred video games to going to the movies, and six times as many preferred video games to renting movies. By the turn of the century, Sony had sold five million boxes a year of its PlayStation brand in the United Kingdom alone.

Online games are, of course, the fastest growing niche in this market. As the Norwegian media researcher Toril Mortensen points out, online computer games in 2006 occupied a very different and more important position in the youth culture than just a decade earlier (Mortensen, 2006). Estimates from 2003 showed that sales from consoles and software reached $17 billion in the United States and Europe alone. Figures from the companies dealing with market analysis of games show that income from subscriptions to online games alone had increased from $500 million in 2002 to $2 billion in 2005, and projections estimate this figure will increase to $6 to 8 billion by 2011. The newest trend is to buy characters and objects in the games for real money. The game *Project Entropia* is linked through a figure of yourself to your own credit card. The most popular games like *Everquest* and *World of Warcraft* are money machines (Stordal, 2006).

So let's face it: video games are not going to go away. Peace researchers therefore need to take the messages of these games more seriously. To do that, we must draw upon the scientific literature on computer gaming (Aarseth, 2001; Miller, 2006; Haddon, 1999; Karlsen, 1998).

Culture of Violence in Computer Games

The quality of video games developed in tandem with the growth of violent content in the games, and the violence has become more and more realistic. *Street Fighter II* was launched in 1991 with a three-dimensional, lifelike character. It featured enormous blue light trails from swishing limbs and fireball attacks, while *Mortal Kombat* from 1992 caused debate among politicians because of its terrifically detailed death moves, in which a victorious character would rip out the opponent's spine and display it triumphantly, with all its bloody details (Poole, 2004). With a "motion capture" technique that films real martial artists and digitizes the results as a movement code that can be applied to the imaginary, game fights between characters and wars are portrayed in an increasingly realistic manner (Ibid.).

Poole suggests why war games have been so successful in the video-game industry. The military logic fits well with the logic of the game itself:

> Armchair generals are well catered for by the God's game's sibling genre, the real-time strategy game. Its natural milieu is that of war. Again in a godlike position (single-handedly overseeing all military operations), the player is briefed by advisers (actors and video clips) and must carry out certain missions by issuing commands to numerous small troop units on the battlefield. The player clicks on a certain unit and, for instance, tells it to move somewhere, to attack another unit, to defend or to scatter (Ibid.).

The successful "Command and Conquer" series offers real historical events explained by the logic to be found in a militaristic approach to history. The game concentrates on the "action" in real "theatres of war." Rather than challenge the player to think in terms of conflict resolution, how to avoid war or achieve peaceful conflict transformation, the game offers hi-tech weaponry with which your troops can pick up and bash the "enemy."

The "winning solutions" of the war games fits well into the concept of war journalism in Galtung's above-mentioned model for war and peace journalism. It's a zero-sum game with two parties and one "winner." The very logic of the game fits well into a Cold War logic with a good and an evil side. The formal root of contemporary games is Atari's panic-inducing arcade game *Missile Command* from 1980. This game originally grew out of a military simulation to see how many nuclear warheads a human radar operator could track before overload set in. As the games became more and more complex and hybridized, the essential elements of real-time strategy (the control of multiple games pieces and tactical calculus) have cropped up in other genres but were originally developed for the war games (Poole, 2004).

The Link between Computer Games and Real War

Evan Wright, the author of the book *Generation Kill*, spent two months living with 23 U.S. Marines from First Recon, the elite unit that spearheaded the invasion of Iraq (2004). In his book, Wright refers to a Marine soldier who talks about the game *Grand Theft Auto: Vice City* at the same time that they are about to attack a unit of alleged insurgents, "I was just thinking one thing when we drove into that ambush: *Grand Theft Auto: Vice City.* I felt like I was living it when I saw the flames coming out of windows, the blown-up car in the street, guys stealing out around shooting at us. It was fucking cool" (quoted in Herbst, 2005).

Wright describes how the violence in video games is related to experiences on the battlefield. He compares the war in Iraq with earlier wars, and concludes that the soldiers seem to be more trigger-happy than previously. With reference to the book *On Killing* by Dave Grossman, Wright makes the point that in past generations only 15 percent to 20 percent of combat infantrymen were willing to fire weapons, whereas in Wright's unit he saw no resistance to firing. He argues that this change of attitude owes something to the experience of violence in entertainment (quoted in Matera, 2005).

In another article, Wright tells how soldiers in the unit were quite open about killing civilians, one even saying that it was authorized by the priest in the unit—so long as they didn't enjoy the killing. Quoting this soldier, Wright writes, "by the time the unit reached the outskirts of Baghdad, this sergeant was certain he had killed at least four men. When this commander praised the unit for 'slaying dragons' on the way to Baghdad, the sergeant later told his men, 'If we did half the shit back home down here, we'd be in prison' " (Wright, 2004b).

The Cooperation between the Military and the Entertainment Industry

Another dimension in the relationship between entertainment and wars is the significance of the strategic cooperation between the military-industrial complex and the entertainment industry. The origin of video games can be traced back to the Cold War, and the technology behind them can be traced back to the U.S. government's nuclear research facility, the Brookhaven National Laboratory, and an engineer who had designed electronic devices for the Manhattan Project's atomic bomb (Herman, 1997). In a 1996 policy paper, the U.S. National Research Council (NRC) acknowledged the importance of cooperation between the Department of Defense (DOD) and the entertainment industry on issues such as modeling and simulation technology. The report makes the following statement: "For DOD, modeling and simulation technology provides a low-cost means of conducting joint training exercises, evaluating new doctrine and tactics, and studying the effectiveness of new weapon systems" (quoted from Burston, 2003).

The significance of this cooperation manifests itself in computer games in the commercial market. In 2002, the game *Desert Storm* was launched, more than ten years after the Gulf War and one year before the next war on Iraq. It could be argued that the timing was not a coincidence; it might be helpful to recreate the sense of winning the war of 1991 in the same country where a new war was going to take place requiring new recruits. To be a winner in this game, you have to act as the American soldiers did in 1991. If you are on the Iraqi side you lose and get killed. What message does this send to young people (mostly boys) in a pre- war situation? (Nohrstedt and Ottosen, 2005).

The Political Economy of the Game Industry[1]

To understand the political and economic roots of the war-game industry, I will draw upon the work of Tim Lenoir (2000). Lenoir's point of departure is that he is intrigued by the notion that we are on the verge of a new renaissance similar to that of the 14th and 15th centuries, deeply connected with a revolution in information technology. But unlike the renaissance of the 14th century, which fostered humanism as one of its achievements, the present renaissance is heralding a post-human era in which the human being is merged with the intelligent machine. As Lenoir puts it, "In the post-human state, there is no demarcation between bodily existence and computer simulation, between cybernetic mechanisms and biological organism" (Lenoir, 2000).

Lenoir links the technological revolution behind the computer game industry to research agencies such as the DARPA (Defense Advanced Research Projects Agency), several private companies, such as Xerox Parc, and research universities. Since 1996, the DARPA Smart Modules program has been developing and demonstrating new ways of combining new technologies (such as microprocessors) with lightweight, low power, module packages to simulate realistic battlefield situations (Ibid.). Lenoir links the military's need to develop simulation and training programs to the entertainment industry, and uses the development of Ivan Sutherland's head-mounted display project as an example of cooperation between the academic and industrial sectors.

The history starts 40 years ago. Sutherland had a Harvard background but funding for the project came from different sources: the military, universities, industry and the CIA. The CIA provided $80,000 in 1966, and funds were also supplied by ARPA, the Office of Naval Research and Bell Labs. The Helicopter company Bell provided equipment, while the Air Force offered up PDP-1 computers. MIT's Lincoln Labs, under an ARPA contract, provided an ultrasonic head-position acoustic sensor, which became an important component in the new video-game technology. In 1968, Sutherland left for Utah, where he joined the computer science department at the University of Utah, which subsequently became an important environment for the development of new computer technology and computer graphics (Ibid.). The new animation technology has also been used in films such as *Jurassic Park* and *Toy Story*. The commercial breakthrough came in 1993, when Silicon Graphics, NEC, and Nintendo announced a partnership, and the world's most powerful game machine was launched. In 1997, the game *Super Mario 64* captured a worldwide base and sold $2-billion worth of games.

The success of *Doom II* led the U.S. Marines to look ahead to the next step in the commercialization of war-games. Cooperation with the company MÄK Technologies led to the design of a tactical operations game built to Marine specifications. According to the contract, the game should eventually go on sale as an official Marine Corps tactical training game. In addition to its work in the defense community, MÄK's software has been licensed for use by several entertainment firms (such as Total Entertainment Network and Zombie Virtual Reality Entertainment) to develop 3-D, multi-user video games such as *Spearhead*. *Spearhead* was published by Interactive Magic and can be played over the Internet, taking distribution a step further. Its networking technology is similar to that used in military simulations. This became a new standard for all Department of Defense simulations, part of a DOD-wide effort to establish a common technical framework to facilitate the inter-operability of all types of models and simulations.

MÄK benefits from working with both the military and commercial markets, taking advantage of the close to $500-million spent by the U.S. government to develop this technology. The contract between MÄK and the Marine Corps led to the contract for *MEU 2000*, a computer-based tactical decision-making game for the Marine Corps as well as a game for the commercial market, a multiplayer game in which each player assumes a position in the command hierarchy of either American or opposing forces. This became a prototype of later games where a military version boasts more accurate details about tactics and weapons than does the civilian. Both versions, however, allow multiple players to compete on the Internet (Lenoir, 2000).

America's Army—a Success Story

One of the biggest successes on a global scale in the computer market is the official U.S. Army computer game (Nieborg, 2006). From the time it was released as *America's Army: Recon* on July 4, 2002 until 2006, it had been upgraded with 22 new versions (Løvlie, 2007). The game comes in different versions, one of which reproduces the image of courageous American soldiers and is available free of charge on the Internet. We can read from the game's introduction on the home page, "The Soldiers in Special Forces are a reflection of the Army within which they serve. They are courageous, intelligent, and resourceful and dedicated individuals." A new version was launched in 2003 (the same year that the invasion in Iraq took place) at the Electronic Entertainment Expo in Los Angeles, May 13-16, in a combination of real and virtual events. Real tanks were placed outside as Air Force Division 101 launched a simulated attack (Pilet, 2003). Inside the Expo, the new game was introduced as a tool to recruit more soldiers to the real U.S. Army at the same time as it was introduced free of charge as a video game on the Internet. By November 2003 it already had 2 to 3 million users; by spring 2007 the number had passed 8 million, ranking among the most popular games on a global scale (Løvlie, 2007).

The question is, of course, why the game is offered free when it has such global market potential. A tool for recruitment in the American market is the most obvious answer. In addition the purpose is to strengthen the image of U.S. Army among the domestic and international public (Løvlie, 2007, 14). In an interview with the Army News Service, Col. Casey Wardynski (director of the OMEA, project director of *America's Army* and associate professor of economics at the U.S. Military Academy) made clear how efficient a tool it is: "The game has generated interest in the Army and has taught people about soldiering," he said. In a survey given to youths aged 16 to 21, 29 percent said that *America's Army* was the most effective method of generating interest (Petemeyer, 2004). Nor should the game be underestimated as a global instrument of propaganda. The game is, of course, extremely one-sided in its approach and offers the military solution as the only solution to a conflict. In addition, all issues are seen through an American perspective.

The Message of *America's Army*

In an attempt to apply rhetorical analysis to the non-verbal text in *America's Army*, Anders Sundnes Løvlie draws inspiration from Roland

Barthes' visual analysis. According to Barthes, the message of the image can be analyzed on three levels, "The linguistic message, the denotative message (or the uncoded, iconic message) and the connotative, cultural or symbolic message, which is seen as coded, iconic message" (Løvlie, 2007). Løvlie found subtle evidence of glorification of U.S.-led warfare implicit in the rhetoric of the game:

> What kind of rhetoric is this? It may seem like a relatively subtle kind of rhetoric, certainly one that deals with "minimal gestures" rather than overwhelming impressions or provocative postures. *America's Army* is propaganda, and there are certainly instances of verbal-text rhetoric of the most patriotic and grandiose kind in the game ... however, the rhetoric of the game form itself, which is the one I have been trying to analyze, doesn't seem to rely on such an overtly excessive language. Instead it is a rhetoric of modesty, responsibility and moral authority; making sure no one may come to see themselves as terrorists killing U.S. soldiers, avoiding unrealistic excesses and undisciplined play (Løvlie, 2007, 108).

America's Army is not the only militaristic game on the market. I could mention *Falcon 4.0* or *Counter Strike* and *Real Wars*. According to Nieborg, "*Counter Strike* was a role model for *America's Army*. One of the newest games, *Full Spectrum Warrior*, was also initially developed as a training game, then recycled and released to the public. It is set in the fictional country Zekistan, whose dictator has been accused of 'ethnic cleansing and terrorist sponsorship'" (2006). Building upon these foundations, an interesting approach would be to analyze whether we find tendencies of what Galtung calls "war journalism," blaming "the other" rather than the war for problems inflicted on people in war zones embedded in the texts of war games.

America's Army: Rise of a Soldier in Light of Galtung's Model

As an experiment to test the hypothesis that Galtung's model for peace journalism could be used on computer games, I selected a group of students with skills in computer games and chose two games, one to be tested towards the "peace journalism" part of Galtung's model and another to be tested with regard to the "war journalism" part of the model. The first game was *Global Conflicts: Palestine* (*GCP*), which is discussed in the subsequent section of this chapter. The latter was *Rise of a Soldier*, a game within the *America's Army* series. The conclusion was that students found the experiment useful to clarify "hidden messages" in the games.[2] Independent of this group report, my research assistant analyzed GCP based on Galtung's model. His findings confirmed the findings from the student group work and will be presented later in the chapter (Ottosen and Wærnes, 2008).

Typical for *America's Army (AA)*, *Rise of a Soldier* stresses individual responsibility, the duty of each soldier to keep the USA "safe." The soldiers in the game are repeatedly challenged on their loyalty toward the nation. Their acts are always framed as defensive, as a response to the threat of terrorism. This fits well into the propaganda-perspective in Galtung's model. These propaganda messages are repeated over and over again in small video-messages and commentaries from your teammates. The game is also clearly ethnocentric with comments that strengthen "othering," such as, "Can anybody understand anything of what these guys are yelling?" The enemy is portrayed as stressed, paranoid, and inarticulate, repeatedly shouting "Bakh, bakh, bakh!" Their primitiveness and dehumanization are underscored by evidence that "they" lack the ability to regroup and work together.

This game fits well into Galtung's model on war journalism, portraying "them" as the problem and "evil doers." The focus in the game is that "we" must stick together against "them." The claim that the United States should be proud to have brave and strong soldiers recurs without context. The acts of the "enemy" are never explained in terms of reasons for fighting or who they actually are as persons. The origin of the conflict is historically unclear and the political and social context of the war is never explained. This us-them perspective, another criterion in Galtung's model for war journalism, is also evident in the structure of the game. It is *your* avatar and *your* team who dominate the scene throughout the game. "Our" side is also more advanced, better equipped with the most modern weapons, and stronger. The game is constructed so that it is easier to eliminate "the enemy" than to kill our own soldiers. Usually the enemy is killed with two or three shots, while "our soldiers" can survive 10 hits. This underlines the hidden message that this is not a battle between "equals."

There is only one goal: to win by "taking out" enemy soldiers. There is no focus on conflict resolution or negotiation and never any motivation to reduce the level of violence. The only action rewarded is violence and killing. There is no room for negotiation or reflection in the game; the only way to move forward is to follow orders and kill the "enemy." If you don't achieve that goal, you fail to qualify to move from the initial "exercise" phase into the actual combat zone phase of the game. This fits well into Galtung's win-oriented approach in the war-journalism model and makes it impossible for the game to serve Galtung's ambition to be "truth-oriented" and supports Løvlie's conclusion quoted earlier (2006). When there are few actual facts in the game, the whole issue of "truth" is mystified.

In the game, buildings blown apart remain as visible evidence of the effect of war, but the human consequences for the civilians and survivors are absent. The human costs of war and death are out of balance and never explained in detail. There is no representation of human loss, no people in grief, no pain. In human terms, the only visible effect of the violent action is on your own avatar. If he is hit, he breathes heavily and the screen goes red. But it is possible to "heal" your avatar by giving certain commands. "The enemy" screams when hit, and there is no way to save him. The conclusion is that Galtung's criteria for war/violence orientation clearly are evident in the game (Brustad et al., 2007).

What Are the Counter Forces?

As I mentioned earlier, the challenge is to develop alternatives—games in the same arena but with a different message, games inspired by the spirit of peace journalism, and which are as entertaining as the war games. It is, of course, hard to compete with the quality of the technology in which the military industrial complex has invested such vast resources as have been documented, but the effort should be made.

Newsgaming

Newsgaming was an attempt by Gonzalo Frasca to create an alternative strategy to meet the challenge from the violent commercial game industry. Through the website www.ludology.org, and the ideology of ludology, an attempt is made to create computer simulators based on actual events such as 9/11 and Madrid, with alternative perspectives on current events. The website itself defines newsgaming thus:

> Newsgaming is a word we coined for describing a genre that is currently emerging: videogames based on news events. Traditionally, videogames have focused on fantasy rather than reality, but we believe that they can be a great tool for better understanding our world. Since newsgaming is so new, it has to find a voice of its own. Therefore, most of our games will be in part experimental.

According to Frasca, "Ludology is most often defined as the study of game structure (or gameplay), as opposed to the study of games as narratives or games as a visual medium" (Frasca, 2003; Tronstad, 2003). According to the Norwegian media researcher Ragnhild Tronstad, Frasca makes a distinction between ludus and paidia rules. Frasca reserves the terms ludus for games that produce winners and losers. "Ludus rules are therefore rules that define a winning situation. Paidia rules are rules that define or restrict the process of playing: how the equipment may be manipulated, for instance" (Tronstad, 2003, 5). Some peace-oriented games have the potential to create a winning situation in favor of peace as an alternative to the propaganda-oriented war games.

To my mind, ludology, and websites such as www.ludology.org offer an interesting platform for creating alternatives to the games coming out of the military industrial complex. *September 11* is a good case study because it fits well into Galtung's model for peace journalism. It has no narrative but is open-ended. The idea is to make visible the consequence, for civilians, of a military solution. If you target an Arabic-looking person equipped with a gun, you are just as likely to hit civilians in the street close to the target. Or you can accidentally hit a civilian target in the city center. There is no winner in this game, but it's evident that a military solution causes a lot of damage. This can stimulate the player to choose alternatives to war. I am in some doubt, however, as to whether this is as exciting, and as attractive as a game, as the more traditional videogames described in this paper.

Global Conflicts: Palestine. One of the most relevant game as a counterforce within the field of war and peace journalism is a game called *Global Conflicts: Palestine (GCP)*, launched in May 2007 and developed by the Copenhagen-based company Serious Games Interactive.[3] On their homepage, the ambition of the project is explained as a desire, "to create computer games that include well-proven game features found in most computer games like action, death and violence but adding an agenda beyond entertainment."[4] *GCP* is certainly a game within the category *edutainment* with the ambition to combine entertainment and fun. *GCP* is about exploring the gameworld, talking to a number of local residents and solving missions along the way. This structure marks *GCP* as a standard "adventure" game, solving the various missions also makes *GCP* a "puzzle" game. The following analysis of the game based on the first point in Galtung's model illustrates the application of Galtung's model to video games (for the complete analysis, see Ottosen and Wærnes, 2008).

The main player in *GCP* has the role of a journalist (either male or female). The game itself begins as the player's character arrives at Jerusalem and meets with her new editor, Henry Fulbright. Fulbright informs the player about the possibilities to visit various places, talk to the people involved in the different incidents and collect quotes that can be used by three different newspapers. These three newspapers are called *Israeli Post, Palestine Today,* and *Global News*, the latter being a European newspaper. Before the start of each mission, the player must choose which of the three newspapers she wants to report to. The quotes gathered from both sides of the conflict (from civilians, soldiers or others) must be used according to the specific agenda of the newspaper chosen.

The Israeli newspaper encourages the player to use quotes that frame Israel as merely defending itself against enemies. The Palestine newspaper, on the other hand, wants stories framing the Palestinians as being suppressed and humiliated, an example being the endless waiting at the checkpoints and harassments from the Israeli soldiers. The European newspaper wants quotes that illustrate the situation for all parties involved, in other words more balanced stories. Under the course of each mission, the player has to choose five quotes that will be used in the story, these quotes (and their conformity with each newspaper's agenda) are the most important aspects of the game in terms of achieving a successful mission.

To get the most useful information out of the people contacted, the player throughout the game must gain trust. Every conversation has a bar that goes from red to green. The player's level of trust is indicated by an arrow placed in the corresponding bar. Asking questions and performing minor tasks (for example delivering a letter, etc.) affect the player's position on the trust bar. The more trust the player has with people, the more stories and quotes will be obtained.

Six different game missions can be played successively. They are called: *Military Raid, The Checkpoint, Mohammad and the Settlers, The Role of the Martyrs,* and *The Other Side of the Coin.*[5] They cover various incidents and situations such as raids against suspected terrorists, managing checkpoints and terrorist attacks. Through these missions the player must choose how to report the different incidents and be mindful as to which questions to address. The success of each mission is measured in a thoughtful way, more specifically, where the newspaper places the story. A medium performance (and story) is rewarded by being placed in the back of the newspaper, whilst close to perfect performance is given the front page. One interesting aspect is that the trust bar is influenced by which side the player has reported for, lowering the level of trust amongst those of the opposite side. One way of leveling this out is by alternately including the two parties or writing for the European newspaper. The question addressed in this essay is whether Galtung's model for peace journalism can be applied usefully to analyze *GCP*'s *The Checkpoint* mission.

The Relevance of Galtung's Model of Peace Journalism

Galtung's first perspective in the peace journalism model—peace/conflict-oriented vs. solution-oriented—consists of eight primary criterias,of which I will use six listed below and apply them to the specific content from *GCP*.

1. *Explore conflict formation, x parties, y goals, z issues, general "win-win" orientation. GCP* does not contain any form of pre-story that describes the ongoing situation. Instead the player is supposed to learn through experience in the field (or playing the game). Conversations with various inhabitants enable the player to learn about the conflict from both sides. Each incident must be understood by the player, and the conversations act as bodies of information that explain what is happening, how people are affected by the situation and which outcome they prefer.

In *The Checkpoint* mission you are sent to a specific checkpoint to cover how they operate, why they are there, and how people are affected by them. Soldiers explain how checkpoints are in place to assure safety, being under constant terrorist attack, etc. Waiting in line is a woman who suddenly faints. As the player rushes to her aid, she reveals that she is pregnant and on her way to a doctor's appointment. Her husband is talking to Israeli soldiers in charge to speed up the procedure. Soldiers, however, tell the player that the checkpoint is practically closed due to a potential terrorist threat, leaving the pregnant woman waiting in the scorching sun. Her husband has no luck with the Israeli soldiers due to the fact that someone in his family is an alleged terrorist. The pregnant woman therefore asks the player for help.

If the player chooses to, he can talk to the soldiers for her. Finally she is permitted through the checkpoint, but her husband has to stay behind for security reasons. Shortly after this, a terrorist rushes towards the checkpoint firing a gun at civilians and soldiers, hurting (and possibly killing) several people. The terrorist is taken down by the Israeli soldiers and ambulances come to the scene. The player then has to find a telephone and submit his story to the chosen newspaper. Although this mission can be regarded as a lose-lose situation, it does give an example of how the game includes all parties, explains their issues and opens the potential for insight into long-term consequences. In the following I will present some finding structured according to six of the points in Galtung's model:

1. *Open space, open time; causes and outcomes anywhere, also in history/culture.* Although the missions in *GCP* are closed in time and space, the conversations with the people involved lead to information about the history of the conflict. This is an important part of understanding the situation as a whole, giving it a historical and cultural context.

2. *Giving voice to all parties; empathy, understanding.* There are various people involved and it's crucial to get an overview of the situation based on the perspectives of all parties involved. Of course, if the player is biased, he can choose to speak with and help only individuals from one party and to tell only their stories, thus neglecting the other side of the conflict. The game itself, however, tries to balance the stories, so as not to promote the views of any of the parties.

3. *See conflict/war as problem, focus on conflict creativity.* There is no doubt that *GCP* sees this conflict as a destructive problem, illustrated by the content in the six missions. People are harassed, killed, attacked by soldiers or terrorists, etc., highlighting the loss of security and human rights. *GCP* relies almost exclusively on conversations/interviews. Often it is necessary to convince people to help the player. An example is the case above when a soldier is confronted with the pregnant woman in need of assistance. *GCP* is trying to show that resolutions can be brought forward by mutual understanding.

4. *Humanization of all sides; more so the worse the weapons.* As *GCP* is not too concerned with the high-end political level of the conflict, it is natural that the conflict is portrayed through the eyes of ordinary people. This helps humanize the conflict as the player is confronted with situations from the ground level. Ordinary Israeli soldiers are worried about terrorist attacks, whilst Palestinians are scared of harassment from Israeli soldiers, for example.

5. *Proactive: prevention before any violence/war occurs.* In *GCP* the player has the possibility of being proactive on a micro level, since the macro level conflict between Israel and Palestine has been active for more than 60 years. The player is not given the role as the savior of peace between the nations, as this would result in a fictitious storyline. The player can, however, mediate in the specific situations, sometimes preventing worse things from happening. One example would be helping the pregnant woman through the checkpoint to prevent her health from deteriorating.

6. *Focus on invisible effects of violence (trauma and glory, damage to structure/culture).* Through conversations with all the different people encountered in *GCP* the player will learn how the conflict has affected

them. Many of them are distrustful of people from the other side, often being a result of a personal experience. Some Palestinians are frustrated over the fact that they cannot go about their usual business without meeting suspicion and harassment. Israelis on the other hand wish they didn't have to worry about suicide bombs or car bombs in their everyday life. *GCP* tries to show how people have been traumatized by the conflict, inflicting paranoia and fear into the mindset of the people living there.

By using Galtung's model of peace journalism, we can see that *GCP* has taken many of the conflict's aspects into consideration. One important aspect is that *GCP* tries to remain impartial, leaving the conclusion in the player's hands. The player, however, has the option of being biased; scoring a front-page for the Israeli or Palestine newspaper that requires biased reporting. *GCP* thereby shows how biased journalism affects the stories that are reported, something that is evident in real-world reporting. This is an important lesson to learn and perhaps the most interesting aspect found in *GCP*.

Conclusion

The game market is a mass market with a variety of attractive offers to fill the spare time of young people. Youth seem reluctant, these days, to spend much time on the news media, and their knowledge about the world comes primarily through entertainment in movies and games. At present, we can only speculate about what kind of worldview young people acquire in the long run, after playing games developed by the military industrial complex.

Even though it is difficult to estimate the impact of these real-war video games on the behavior of the users, the content should nevertheless be analyzed in terms of war propaganda. The digital technology emerging from the research laboratories in the military-industrial complex serves as a simulator, preparing soldiers for real wars, whereas the same technology—and in many cases the same games—is also converted into commercial video games. The long-term impact of millions of users playing within the narrative of war propaganda is unclear. Some disturbing evidence from the battlefield in Iraq suggests that the violent male culture of the video games inspires soldiers to more inhuman and violent behavior on the battlefield.

The economic, technological and cultural links between the entertainment industry and the defense industry make it highly unlikely the major news channels will serve as a critical watchdog in issues of war and peace. Not only are the major news organizations reluctant to criticize the Pentagon and the White House in war preparation, but in some cases they use the same digital technology as the game industry in their news reporting in a manner that blurs the line between fact and fiction in military affairs. Robin Andersen has introduced the notion of the military-entertainment complex to explain the symbiotic relationship between Pentagon and parts of the game industry (Andersen, 2006). The introduction of games like *Global Conflicts: Palestine* offers an alternative for those who want to use computer games as a tool to explore new approaches to peace building and conflict resolution.

The hope is that peace researchers inspired by the analytical tools offered in the concept of peace journalism, and game designers inspired by ludology, can create a counter force and promote popular games based on peace-building and non-violence. The suggestion of this study is that Johan Galtung's model for war and peace journalism can be a useful tool in analyzing computer games. The model offers an analytical tool that can be used to raise awareness of the war-oriented, ethnocentric and propagandistic character of the games coming out of the military industrial complex. It remains to be seen whether alternatives to games generated by the military-entertainment complex can be commercially sustainable.

Notes

1. Parts of this section will also be published in Ottosen 2008.
2. The students conducting the experiment published a report as a part of their bachelor thesis in Media and Communication at Oslo University College, see Brustad et al., 2007.
3. The students in this experiment also analyzed this game and research assistant Daniel Wærnes conducted a separate in-depth analysis of the game. Many thanks to Daniel Wærnes. I draw heavily upon his analysis and writing in this part of the article (Ottosen and Wærnes, 2008).
4. http://www.seriousgames.dk/new/about.php.
5. There is just room for presenting parts of the analyses here. The full report from the study is presented in Ottosen and Wærnes 2008.

References

Aarseth, Espen. 2001. "Computer Games Studies, Year One." In *Game Studies. The International Journal of Computer Game Research*, 1(1).
Andersen, Robin 2006. *A Century of Media. A Century of War.* New York: Peter Lang.
Artz, Lee and Yaha R. Kamalipour (eds.) 2005. *Bring 'Em On.* New York: Rowman & Littlefield.
Bagdikian, Ben H. 2004. *The New Media Monopoly.* Boston: Beacon Press.
BBC. 2006. Story from BBC NEWS:http://news.bbc.co.uk/go/pr/fr/-/2/hi/technology/6059026.stm. Published: 2006/10/18 07:34:26 GMT

Brustad, Caroline, Brygard, Andrea B., Dyrseth, Kristin K. and Gabrielsen, Siri. 2007. "Ideologi og føring i dataspil" Fordypningsoppgave Medier og kommunikasjon, Høgskolen i Oslo.

Burston, Jonathan. 2003. "War and Entertainment Industries: New research Priorities in an Era of Cyber-Patriotism" in Thussu, Daya Kishan & Freedman, Des (eds.) 2003. *War and the Media*. London: Sage publications.

Frasca, Gonzalo. 2003. "Simulation versus Narrative: Introduction to Ludology in Wolf, J.P. and Perron (eds.) *The Video Game Theory Reader*. New York: Routledge.

Galtung, Johan. 1990. "Cultural violence." In *Journal of Peace Research*, 27(3), August, pp. 291-305.

Galtung, Johan. 2002. "Peace journalism—a challenge." In Kempf, Wilhelm and Heikki Loustarinen (eds.) *Journalism and the New World Order, Vol. 2. Studying the War and the Media*. Gothenburg: Nordicom.

Greenfield, Patricia. 1984. *Media and the Mind of the Child. From Print to Television, Videogames and Computers*. Cambridge: Harvard University Press.

Haddon, Leslie. 1999. "The development of interactive games." In Mackay, Hugh and Tim O' Sullivan (eds.) *The Media Reader: Continuity and Transformation*. London: Sage.

Herbst, Claudia. 2005. "Shock and awe. Virtual females and the sexing of war." In *Feminist Media Studies* 5(3).

Herman, Leonard. 1997. *The Fall and Rise of Videogames*. 2nd ed. New Jersey: Rolenta Press.

Holen, Øyvind. 2006. Redder verden med joystick. In *Ny Tid* No. 26, 7. July 2006.

Karlsen, Faltin. 1998. *Dataspill og vold. En kvalitativ analyse av voldsbruk i dataspill*. Statens filmtilsyn.

Lenoir, Tim. 2000. "All but war is simulation: The Military-Industrial Complex." In *Configurations* 8. The John Hopkins University Press and the Society for Literature and Science.

Loftus, Geoffrey R., and Elisabeth F. Lofthus. 1983. *Mind and Play: The Psychology of Videogames*. New York: Basic Books.

Løvlie, Anders Sundnes 2007. "The rhetoric of persuasive games. Freedom and discipline in America's Army." Master thesis in media science, Department of Media and Communication, University of Oslo.

Lynch, Jake, and Annabel McGoldrick 2005. *Peace Journalism*. Stroud: Hawthorne Press.

Matera, Angelo 2005. "Into Iraq With 'Generation Kill' ": An Interview with Evan Wright. *God Spy*, 30 December. http://www.godspy.com/reviews/Into-Iraq-With-Geenration-Kill-Interview-with-E ...

Nieborg, David B. 2006. " 'We want the whole world to know how great the U.S. Army is!'—Computer Games and Propaganda," in Manthos Santorineos (ed.): *Gaming Realities—A Challenge for Digital Culture*. Athens: Fournos.

Miller, Toby. 2006. "Gaming for beginners." In *Games and Culture,* 1(1), 2006.

Mortensen, Toril Elvira. 2003. *Pleasures of the Player: Flow and Control in Online Games*. Doctoral Thesis Department of Humanistics, University of Bergen and Faculty of Media and Journalism, Volda University College.

Mortensen, Toril Elvira. 2006. WoW is the New MUD: Social Gaming from Text to Video. In *Games and Culture* No. 1, 2006.

Nohrstedt, Stig A. and Rune Ottosen. 2005. (eds.). *Global War – Local News. Media Images of the Iraq War.* Gothenburg: Nordicom.

Ottosen, Rune. 2007. "Emphasising images in peace journalism: Theory and practice in the case of Norway's biggest newspaper." In *Conflict & Communication Online*, No. 2 Spring 2007.

Ottosen, Rune. 2008. "Targeting the Player: Computer Games as Propaganda for The Military-Industrial Complex." Under publication in *Nordicom Review*.

Ottosen, Rune, and Wærnes, Daniel. 2008. Analysis of Global Conflicts: Palestine-unpublished working paper (in the files of the author).

Pilet, Stephane. 2003. "Dataspill som propagandavåpen." *Le Monde diplomatique* (Norwegian edition) September 2003.

Petemeyer, Kelli. 2004. Online Army Recruiting Reaches Top 5 List. Army News Service.

Poole, Steven. 2004. *Trigger Happy. Videogames and the Entertainment Revolution.* New York: Arcade Publishing.

Stordal, Hans Ivar. 2006. "Fantasi som vekstøkonomi" In *Ny Tid* 20 1, June 2006.

Thomas, Tanja, and Virchow. 2005. "Banal militarism and the culture of war." In Artz, Lee and Yaha R. Kamalipour (eds.) *Bring 'Em On.* New York: Rowman & Littlefield.

Tronstad, Ragnhild. 2003. "Defining a Tubmud Ludology" in www.dichtung-digital. org/2003/4-tronstad.htm.

Wright, Evan. 2004. *Generation Kill.* New York: Putnam.

Wright, Evan. 2004b. "Dead-Check in Falluja. Embedded with the Marines in Iraq." In *The Village Voice*, November 24-30, 2004.

Psychological Effects of War Journalism and Peace Journalism

Annabel McGoldrick

Peace Journalism

Peace journalism, as elaborated by a growing number of its proponents, practitioners and analysts, is an approach to the news representation of conflicts which is:

- Peace-orientated;
- Truth-orientated;
- People-orientated; and
- Solution-orientated.

In the original schema by Johan Galtung (in Lynch and McGoldrick, 2005, 6), peace journalism is contrasted with war journalism, which is orientated:

- Towards violence;
- Towards propaganda;
- Towards elites; and
- Towards victory.

Lynch and McGoldrick (2005) have set out the baseline normative theoretical assumptions from the discipline of peace and conflict studies, which underpin these distinctions. Research into conflict dynamics has turned up several persistent themes, they say:

- Violence is never wholly its own cause—conflict is made up of structure, culture, and process—the context, without which no explanation for a violent event is complete or, indeed, correct.
- Non-violent responses are always possible. There is always more than one way of responding to conflict. Many people, in many places, are devising, advocating and applying non-violent responses.

- More than two sides—there are always more than two parties to any conflict— some, whose involvement or interest is hidden, need putting on the map, others, presented as a solid aggregate of view, may contain important internal divisions, and they need *dis*-aggregation.
- Every party has a stake—parties to conflict should be seen as stakeholders, pursuing their own goals, needs and interests—some openly acknowledged, but almost invariably some hidden as well (Ibid., xviii).

Peace journalism, therefore, is likely to include material on the background of conflict, showing direct violence as an intelligible, if dysfunctional, response to identifiable conditions in social reality. It is likely to highlight non-violence as an alternative response people make, or can make, to the same situation. It seeks and represents a multiplicity of dividing lines, as well as potential for common ground, among conflicting parties, and it interrogates stated agendas and self-presentations, providing clues and cues for readers and audiences to negotiate their own readings of propaganda.

Building upon such distinctions, Kempf (2005) found significant differences between cognitive responses among the same subjects to newspaper articles containing elements of content categorized as "escalation" and to three rewritten versions of the same articles "(a) with increased escalation-oriented framing, (b) with moderate de-escalation oriented framing and (c) with more determined de-escalation oriented framing of the events." Szabo and Hopkinson (2007) also examined the effects of media exposure. Their study exposed a group of undergraduate students to television news bulletins and found that "anxiety and total mood disturbance increased, whereas positive affect decrease ... after watching the news" to the extent that "a directed psychological intervention such as progressive relaxation" was needed to "buffer" the impact (57).

In contrast to this quantitative study, using pre-determined interview protocols, Serlin (2006) used a narrative and archival research method based on "open-ended questions about ... symptoms and experiences" (146) to investigate the effect of media coverage of the war on Iraq on a group of three psychotherapy clients who were Vietnam veterans. Finding that the exposure exacerbated their symptoms of Post-Traumatic Stress Disorder (PTSD), the author recommended that "psychologists be trained to identify and work with ... environmental and cultural factors such as media and politics [as] stressors ... on the psyches of their clients" (Ibid.).

Given the observed differences in cognitive responses to news items adjusted so as to correspond with the distinctions in the peace journalism schema, and the measurable psychological responses to television news bulletins as stressors, this study attempts to combine elements of the two to explore any differentials in the *respective* psychological impact of war journalism and peace journalism on the viewer. In this research, interview subjects watched two versions of the same story, a bus bombing in Jerusalem in August 2003, which form the opening section of *News from the Holy Land*, a film by peace journalism practitioners and educators, Jake Lynch and Annabel McGoldrick (2004). Each version is structured and presented as a piece of television journalism resembling actual international news reporting of the Israeli-Palestinian conflict. The first exhibits framing and discursive characteristics typical of war journalism. The reporter's opening voiceover script:

> Carnage on the streets of Jerusalem—the worst suicide bombing here in more than a year. Israelis in despair that they can ever be safe in their homes. Members of this Orthodox Jewish community already raising calls for Arabs to be forcibly moved out of the East Jerusalem, the border just a few hundred yards from the scene of the blast. Rescue workers pulling survivors from the wreckage and collecting whatever pieces they could find of the dead.

The dualistic orientation of war journalism is clearly evident in this selection, as an opening gambit of the most extreme perspective calling for ethnic cleansing as a response to the bombing. The report goes on to show the bomber's suicide video, clutching a rifle in one hand and a copy of the Qu'ran in the other—"this, the man responsible for the horror.... The extremist group, Hamas, sent him out to kill; in revenge, they said, for attacks on their leaders," the voiceover says. Then the reporter appears in vision to offer the following assessment:

> This devastating blow shattered a period of relative calm here, when progress on the latest peace plan, the American-sponsored roadmap began to seem possible. Now any prospect of peace between Israelis and Palestinians appears as faint and distant as it's ever been.

The conclusion is that "Abu Mazen, the beleaguered Palestinian Prime Minister" now faces "renewed pressure to crack down on militant groups." Speakers included a government official, Avi Pazner, on the Israeli side, threatening reprisals against the Palestinians, and a Hamas spokesman, Ismail Abu Shanab.

The piece conforms to the war journalism side of the Galtung schema. It explains an act of direct violence as revenge for previous direct violence, what Galtung calls a "zero-sum orientation" (in Lynch and McGoldrick, 2005). There is no mention of structure, culture or process. In deciding to include only political leaders, rehearsing familiar slogans, as its speakers, the piece is elite-orientated, and in its implication that peace talks were progressing in a "period of calm" until the bombing interrupted them, it reproduces war propaganda familiar from countless pronouncements by the Israeli and, indeed, U.S. governments. The message is that the Palestinians are to blame; therefore, the solution is to do something to them; hence the need for a "crackdown."

The contrasting second version opens by suggesting that a shared problem—the conflict—is to blame for what has happened:

> Another day of mourning in Jerusalem. A bus carrying families back from a prayer visit to the Old City, when the bomb went off. A high proportion of those killed were children—as if to emphasise the indiscriminate power of this conflict to destroy the lives and hopes of young and old alike.

The script for the reporter's in-vision "stand-up" in this version is very different from the first:

> Israelis and Palestinians are now trapped in a cycle of violence. The elaborate security and military apparatus designed to protect Israel inflicts a steady trickle of casualties on Palestinians. And every time the Palestinians lash out, as one did here, there's a crackdown, making the conditions in which they live still more onerous.

In this, it echoes Galtung's exculpatory nature-structure-culture model:

> A structure-oriented perspective converts the relation from inter-personal, or inter-state/nation, to a relation between two positions in a deficient structure. If the parties can agree that the structure was/is deficient and that their behaviour was an enactment of structural positions rather than anything more personal, then turning together against the common problem, the structural violence, should be possible. A culture-oriented perspective also converts the relation from interpersonal, or inter-state/nation, to a relation spurred by a deficient culture (Galtung, nd).

To represent a conflict as a shared problem, then, is the first step towards resolving it. Speakers include Avi Pazner (the same clip as in the first version) but also a hospital doctor from Qalqilya, representing Palestinians, and a group of Israeli peace activists.

The latter are from a Checkpoint Watch group and are used to illustrate the fallacy in the U.S./Israeli propaganda line that a cease-fire by Hamas and Islamic Jihad, intended to maintain an atmosphere conducive to peace talks, saw a "period of calm." In fact, this report points out, 21 Palestinians had been killed, according to the Red Crescent, in the cease-fire period alone—mainly in incidents at checkpoints. "Progress [in the talks] has been slow," the reporter remarks, "and now risks going into reverse." It is not, or not merely, that a violent incident impedes political progress; a lack of political progress in tackling issues of structural violence, chiefly the armed occupation of Palestinian land, is the indispensable context for understanding and explaining violent incidents.

At the same time, the doctor and the activists represent the possibility of non-violent responses in keeping with Lederach's (1997) observation about the ubiquity of peace as part of the conflict picture, albeit one that is often overlooked (94). Peace journalism "makes audible and visible the subjugated aspects of reality" (Galtung, in Lynch and McGoldrick, 2005), thereby pointing to a possible way out of the conflict "trap" to which the second reporter refers.

Subjects and Methods

Subjects for the present study were all U.K.-based professionals, albeit they originated from several different parts of the country and from different countries—including Northern Ireland, Uganda, and Pakistan. They were selected to represent a range of ethnic origins, and the group comprised seven women and four men. Most participants already had some interest in conflict and the media; and several were encountered at a peace journalism workshop. Others were students in a post-graduate psychotherapy course who had volunteered to participate. Each was interviewed at his or her own home at a time arranged so they would be comfortable and in a relaxed general frame of mind.

The purpose of this study was to obtain a deeper understanding of the human experience of learning about world events, second-hand, as it were, from journalists. Open-ended interview questions were formulated to elicit accounts of personal experience with a minimum of constraint on the participants' responses. Although quantitative methods, of the kind applied in the Szabo and Hopkinson study, were considered, they were not employed because they rely, unavoidably, on pre-scripted interview protocols that limit respondent flexibility to permit tallies of particular responses. Hence the interviews were conducted using a grounded theory approach (Barrell et al., 1987). This method, first developed by Glaser and Strauss (1967), is described by Hiles (2002a) as follows:

> Rather than starting with a prediction, a theory, or a hypothesis to be tested, the researcher is encouraged not to review the literature in any depth, but to approach the research question with an open mind, and allow the theory to emerge from the data that is being collected (3).

Etherington (2004) issues an important caution about the researcher's own biases when collecting such data, "To be reflexive we need be aware of our personal responses and to be able to make choices about how to use them. We also need to be aware of the personal, social and cultural contexts in which we live and work to understand how these impact the ways we interpret our world" (2004). In this case, due reflexivity demanded that allowances be made for the fact that I am "in favor of" peace journalism and that several subjects either already knew this or could deduce it from what they knew of me (albeit none of them had seen this material before). As a precaution against interviewer bias, the following short section of the transcript shows one interviewee in the study, identified as AD, responding to the war journalism version, in which:

- Questions are open-ended and elicitive; and
- Suggestions or prompts in questions are confined to explicit cues already given by the subject in the previous answer.

Question: What effect does it have on you, watching that?

AD: I stop hearing the words. I'm watching facial expressions, noticing things like what label [the reporter] has on his shirt. And that's stopping me from, there's nothing to engage with. It reminds me of when I was in Jerusalem because of the garb that the orthodox Jews are wearing but it doesn't relate beyond that to my experience of being there.

Question: When you say it doesn't relate, in what way does it not relate?

AD: Because I was never there when they had more violent incidents. Some were quite busy and bustling but basically peaceful and people of all different kinds getting along sharing the same space.

Question: Does it not make you more interested because it's somewhere you have spent time, where you've met people?

AD: Initially yes, but then I phase out because of the paciness, the paciness is too much, it's relentless.

Question: What, the information is relentless?

AD: Yes punchy (laughs) even if and then we are chopping, we're chopping from talking to Hamas spokesman (blows repeatedly) phew, phew. And then stuff like Abu Mazen, doesn't know which way to turn. Oh, that just makes me cringe. Because then I am realising it that's set up. It is contrived.

Question: What about the reporter's words—are they contrived?

AD: Also I noticed, they are "calling it the massacre of the children." And I thought are they, or are you? It sounds like a headline.

Question: What about the pictures, how did they affect you?

AD: To be honest I've seen so much of it, it's here we go again, more disaster footage, really I don't care, even though it's somewhere I've been but there's a limit. I feel there's a limit to how much I can care about and that is in jeopardy so I don't want to load on caring too much about everything that the news is throwing at me.

Question: Even though it's somewhere that you've been?

AD: I think because I have been there I would make a point of watching a documentary.

Question: Something that went deeper?

AD: And engaging in conversation with real people if there's some comment about Israel I will put in my tuppence worth if things are relevant.

After some initial general discussion with each participant about the feelings triggered by general experiences of watching, reading and listening to news, the "two versions" of the news story were shown using a laptop computer. Each subject watched the war journalism version first, then the peace journalism version—i.e., in the order in which they appear in the film. Interviews were recorded, using a small, hand-held recording device, and later transcribed.

Data was analyzed using interpretative phenomenological analysis (IPA) to interpret meanings embedded in the texts thus produced, but applying a hermeneutical, rather than textual discourse analytical method: "Discourse analysis regards verbal reports as behaviors in their own right, which should be the focus of functional analysis. IPA, by contrast is concerned with cognitions, that is, with understanding what the particular respondent thinks or believes about the topic under discussion" (Smith, Jarman, and Osborn, 1999). IPA led to the following basic procedural stages: looking for themes in individual interviews; identifying emergent themes across interviews; looking for connections and the clustering of themes; identifying major themes and sub-themes; continuing the analysis through all the interviews until all themes have been fully explored and interconnected (Hiles, 2002b, 5). The analysis across interviews allowed for variation in themes but also looked explicitly for elements common across the participants' experiences.

Following Janesick (2000), triangulation, improvisation, and crystallization were used to refine and evolve interview questions and approaches as the data collection progressed from one subject to the next. This meant approaching the study "using several different facets"; several different methodological approaches, data sources, theories and disciplines to help substantiate the trustworthiness of the inquiry. "This allows for multiple ways of framing the problem, selecting research strategies and extending discourse across several fields of study" (Ibid., 395).

To aid comparison of the results, highlights from the responses to each version are presented as a table, with salient comments quoted directly and important words in bold.

Themes

From the responses summarized here, four dominant themes emerged. The war journalism version was generally found:

1. Harder to listen to;
2. Liable to lead to a sense of disconnection or "switching off";
3. Generative of strong feelings of sadness and hopelessness; and
4. Lacking in context and balance.

The peace journalism version was:

1. Easier to listen to;
2. Replete with opportunities to "connect" with the story, even learn something new;
3. Refreshing and more hopeful; and
4. In a word used by nine out of the 11 interviewees—balanced.

Two of these themes in particular—numbers two and three, the extent and nature of the feeling of "connection" with the news, and the availability of cues enabling the viewer to decode the story in ways that leave room for hope—appear, from an examination of the data, to have implications for psychological well-being; implications differentiated, therefore, on the basis of distinctions between the war journalism and peace journalism modes of representation.

To consider, first, the connection the news invites and enables people to make with the outside world it purports to represent, several interviewees referred in different ways to how the news stops them from thinking. Two said it felt "like my brain has been emptied" and it "decreases consciousness." One said news makes "the realm of the ordinary [become] less available" because it is about "dramas" and "highs and lows" so it is harder to identify with the space in between. Research suggests this effect is exacerbated by the characteristic binary framing of war journalism in which extreme perspectives are likely to receive attention.

Others described this same mechanism as setting up an addiction: "It's a bit like a sugar hit, you want to actively make yourself something that can't be switched off by constantly hitting only the high notes." Another subject used a different analogy, imagining the time when early human beings were being hunted by wildlife on the African plains, 20,000 years ago, and reminding me of Daniel Goleman's "limbic news" argument (Goleman, 1996). The imperative of survival means we are wired to get a hit from fear, and war journalism often sells itself on fear (Lynch, 2008). Instead of sugar, he likened news to hamburgers. For most of human existence, supplies of fat and salt were at a premium, so we would take as much as we could find. Now, we do not have the same food short-ages, and so the danger is of making ourselves ill with too much. But our reptilian brains haven't quite "got" that and we still have a craving for both. "So much of the news agenda is McNews, it appeals to our baser survival instincts … it doesn't actually serve us any more in evolutionary terms in the 21st century."

News may answer the human needs for belonging and security (Maslow, 1970), but it may do so by taking us back and forth "across the threshold" of these needs over and over again, de-sensitizing us so that ever-more "extreme" or shocking news is needed to achieve the same "high." Three subjects named their fear that exposure to the news would lead to them losing their sensitivity, hence their need to protect themselves from such material.

What, then, of the "lows"—the lingering feelings of depression, helplessness, hopelessness and alienation named by several? These are all very negative feelings that impact on our psyche and seep through to our every engagement with people, places and things. One subject described a state of "depression … on and off" over a ten-year period, which she attributed to consuming news about conflict: "I realised that I was depressed because of the war, that in a sense it had really taken over my mind." This was a turning point in her consumption of the media. She linked the depression, in part, to a "growing sense of impotence" and a feeling of despair that she could not do anything to change the world. Others commented that, no matter how much we hear about the Israeli-Palestinian conflict, "nothing changes."

Another subject went on to talk about "compassion fatigue" (Moeller, 1999), an element of cognitive responses that may help to explain why people "switch off"—they are not being given any indication of the dif-ference they can make by caring. The hopelessness thus feeds back in to the sense of disconnection. Psychologist Geoff Scobie remarks that moral fatigue and exhausted empathy are, to some degree, a survival mecha-nism: "When we see fairly horrendous pictures that upset us emotionally

Table 1
War Journalism and Peace Journalism Responses

Subject	War Journalism (WJ) response	Peace Journalism (PJ) response
AD	"The first one felt more like sensation at any cost." "I phase out because of the paciness," "there's nothing to engage with," "I felt I know I should care but I really don't …"	"Felt more like a striving after the truth." She found it easier to listen because it was "stood back." "I felt more hopeless" because both sides were trapped in a cycle of violence. "… but the second one yes, I did care."
LP	Could not listen because she was "cross" with the reporter's "pompous" summary, "how are you going to understand a complicated situation in that length of time?"	"Much more balanced." Found reporter's voice easier to listen to, "your voice was of an explanatory kind of tone. Which wasn't trying to shut down thought but was trying to open out and give as much information as you possibly could in such a short period of time."
IA	"Felt a bit hopeless … very sad …" "It does really seem like an impasse that nobody can ever overcome. Yeah, it's a hopeless case."	Suggested, "balanced" without using the word: "It just gives you a much bigger picture, doesn't it? By contrast it's outrageous that so much is reported in such a one-sided fashion."
NA	Expressed the most pronounced feeling response. Felt helpless and immense sadness for what happened to the Jews and as if all Muslims would be blamed: "I feel my goodness how will I go out people who will watch this news, what impression will they get about [me]?"	"Very balanced" and "it's closer to reality" and this version made her feel empowered to do something. "Like after watching I don't feel this is an attack on me as a Muslim," "be more active," "I can connect with those people."
SA	"Blood, blood, blood, blood all over the place, revenge, revenge and it goes on and on." "This is like planting the hatred in the faces of innocent children and they will never know the truth, it's really heartbreaking."	"Balanced" (uses word 4 times). "My heart rate goes down a little bit because at least I see something a little bit different." He says this version gives context, explains some of the why, which contributes to transforming the situation.
RC	Made him "feel quite sick," "part of me switched off coz I was staying with just the image," felt numb, then felt angry "I felt connected to the victims" but also detached that it was happening "over there and not here."	Made him connect more with the Palestinians. Offered context, why and gave him new info about the Israeli women monitoring the checkpoints.

Table 1 (cont.)

RL	Sad, depressed, numb "I've gone into defence about trying not to get too emotionally involved." Made some interesting comments about Jake and what he heard in his voice, "some sadness in his voice, almost a sense of resignation, him not wanting to be there and be involved in this either, it might have been very subtle but it was there. But also a sense of his humanity and the fact that he was in some way emotionally engaged with the material."	"It was more even-handed. I recognise it was a rounded picture." But that it didn't change his feelings or views because he knew the situation well. "Yes it was deadening in that sense. But the second one was also deadening but in a different way because of a sense of futility and hopelessness that seemed to come across more strongly in the second one."
NP	"Good guys and bad guys." It made her feel hopeless. "On the one hand it is calling you to do something by pulling at that part of you, 'Isn't this a terrible thing that is happening to the little Jewish children?' but on the other hand it creates a sense of hopelessness because I'm so far away what could I possibly do?"	"Balanced" (used the word 4 times). "I have learned something new" about the conflict. "It was really interesting to hear from the woman who puts herself at the checkpoint every day, and pretty much she's one of those faceless people of a conflict so I found that really interesting."
RK	Felt the Israelis were being painted as the goodies and the Palestinians as the baddies.	"More positive and gave hope for the future—it took a more balanced view and you looked at different ways it might be resolved."
RA	WJ was like most stories he saw on Israel with no context leading people to think all Muslims are "crazy terrorists." Makes him sad that people think that about Muslims and sad for the victims.	"Much more balanced" because it gave some context & explanation for violence, "…so if people understand the Israel/ Palestine context better it will impact on their overall image on Islam and Muslims." "Refreshing."
DF	Felt it was biased in favour of the Israelis and she wanted to hear more about why the Palestinians did it. "quite militarish" Graphic images: "I get overwhelmed with it too much and it stays in my head it really does stay in my head."	"Balanced" "Much better." "I didn't feel as if I was being kind of bushwhacked into thinking Israelis are ok and they're the golden people, no they do the most atrocious things and that piece showed it." "I did feel more hopeful," "there were tendrils going out."

... we have some sort of mechanism which prevents us getting quite so emotionally upset the next time we see something" (in Moeller, 1999).

Much of the interview material reflected people's sense of frustration with the news. They looked to it to equip them to make sense of world events, but found it lacking. There was a considerable amount of anger about this, which I interpreted as arising from an unfulfilled human need to be able to make meanings in our lives. News extends our consciousness beyond what is happening in our immediate circles of family, friends, work and community, to the world at large; but the way it *represents* the world denies us the material necessary to make meanings in this larger circle.

Several subjects referred to the psychological impact of news in shaping their relationships with themselves as well as the wider world. One said, "Part of the construction of who we are happens in relation to media.... I think the media is much more powerful in constructing individuals' relationships to self." Another said it "profoundly shapes my internal structure," and several referred to the media being the locus for "working out our morality." In other words media representations enter our interiority, or "narrative of selfhood" (Seigel, 2005). For one woman, there was a greater impact on her sense of security and belonging. She said, "What's reported on Israel ... profoundly shapes my internal psychic structure both in terms of whether I feel identified or whether I feel got at or I feel betrayed or my kind of anxiety about how high-profile it is."

In other cases, respondents felt the need to react against news representations. Several studies have found war journalism to be the majority, even dominant form, in most journalism, in most places, most of the time (Lynch, 2006; Lee and Maslog, 2005; Lee et al., 2006). War journalism is characterized by glimpses of adversarial positions in a dualistic conflict picture that tend to represent the world as polarized. Given that Muslims, for example, are now the subject of such polarization, if people are, indeed, creating their psychic structures around the news, then they may find themselves implicitly on the defensive in their dealings with fellow citizens, as if bound to demonstrate that they themselves can be distinguished from extreme jihadis. Thus, for example, a Muslim respondent said, "People watching that [the war journalism version of the Jerusalem bombing] will just think Muslims are crazy terrorists, nutcase extremist type people. If I was watching this stuff, I [too] would have a fairly negative image of Islam." This is an effect of war journalism to which peace journalism offers what is—the data suggests—at least a partial therapy.

Discussion

Relevant literature suggests that news does not—indeed cannot—tell it "the way it is." Meaning is not fixed before representation but afterwards (Hall, 1997) and, in news, this implicates us, as readers, listeners and viewers, in a dysfunctional relationship with the world around us—dysfunctional because of the conventions of news, which have developed in response to commercial and political interests (Bagdikian, 2000). News is a significant factor in shaping the collective unconscious, which it does by reproducing recognizable myths and archetypes. However, the dominant war journalism conventions mean that these familiar signs and narratives occur in distorted and broken forms that re-inscribe hegemonic social and political narratives (Lule, 2001).

Serlin's clients experienced worsening PTSD symptoms during the Iraq war. The Vietnam veterans were angry about the "political spin," "arbitrary realities" (Serlin 2006) and the meaninglessness of death. Subjects in the present study encountered similar frustrations: an anger with the constructedness of the news; its failure to equip us to make meaning and its "disconnect" with people's lives. They "mistrusted" the news; some felt journalists "misreport," "misrepresent" and "twist the truth." They saw something hollow in its representations. Yes, some were ultimately able to put these insights to constructive use; one participant struck a keynote, however, with the observation that constantly mistrusting the news was a "lost position"—one of alienation, "of not knowing where you are with anything." As Serlin says, "it distorts our most fundamental sense of what it means to be human" (2006).

Several subjects explained how they switched off, literally or internally, through their own experience of compassion fatigue. Heidegger, May suggests, "made care (*sorge*) the basis of being: without care, our selves shrink up, we lose our capacity to will as well as our selfhood" (May 1991). News begins with the premise that we care, or at least should care—which is why we are hearing about the situation in the first place—but it then gives us a long list of problems with no opportunities for us to *apply* our care; most news offers at best superficial explanations of why things are happening, so we cannot discern the shape of any lasting solution, still less how we might contribute to bringing it about. This is, in Maslow's terms, a denial of our human need for self-actualization (1970).

Hall (1997) offers further insight into this mechanism—that news challenges us to be involved, but, while it appears to make events present through the report, it actually confirms their absence. Several subjects said the news wanted something from them, "What am I supposed to *do* with this?" one woman asked four times. Media want us to identify, to be arrested and feel that the news image has "something for you here," and it does that by involving us in the process of constructing meaning.

> The meaning that you as a spectator take depends on that engagement—psychic, imaginary engagement—through the look with an investment in the image or involvement in what the image is saying or doing. So then, whereas we have a notion, in the way in which we talk about images, that images flood us and barrage us with meanings; as if we can stand outside of them and allow them to be there.... We're not bothered because we are barraged by something, which means nothing to us. We are bothered precisely by the fact that we are caught. We do have an investment, in the meaning, which is being taken from it" (Hall, 1997).

This was the experience of one subject who did not want to hear any more about Rwanda because he said it was "too complicated" and its sheer scale meant that, if he did take it on, it threatened to become one of the main projects of his life. We turn away, and that process leaves us with a gap—a void within.

But the other process to which Hall alerts us is the attempts by "power" through journalism to *fix* meaning—in Hall's words "to naturalize representation to the point where you cannot see that anyone produced it" (1997). In other words to agree, "That's the way it is." In the case of the war journalism, to agree that Palestinians are the problem, they are "baddies" and must be removed, punished, or both. But, by showing the second, peace journalism version I alerted participants to the constructedness of the first; I subverted the representation. Indeed, the results must be viewed with this in mind—by the time subjects were responding to the second version, they knew there *were* two versions, and this itself clearly has an effect on their process of decoding.

Most felt "empowered," energized and "hopeful" and several commented that they "learned" something new. Meaning was opened back up, and perhaps, in therapy terms, that is why it feels more satisfying. Viewers are not being made complicit in fixing "arbitrary realities." Being implicated in the production of meaning, especially in war journalism representations of cases like the invasion of Iraq or the "war on terror," actually makes the viewer/reader feel complicit in condoning killing. This is what disturbs and infuriates people and, in some cases, as Serlin (2006) observed, triggers PTSD. We are disturbed because we are drawn into a conspiracy of meaning-making, which now saturates our environment.

The task for therapy is to help clients in finding a sense of what it means to be human in a digital age of information overload (Toffler, 1970). Therapy's job already is to unfix meaning—the core of so many approaches like Gestalt, Existential, and Cognitive Behavioral Therapy, to name but a few. They challenge the client's perspective, to make a different interpretation of events. But such a challenge still does not generally go beyond the intrapsychic circles of the family. To do so would be to carry out the task for therapy set down by its founders, Freud—who wrote about the "understanding ... of the great social institutions" (1953/1975) built from the couch, and Jung:

> This critical state of things has such a tremendous influence on the psychic life of the individual ... he [the analyst] feels the violence of its impact even in the quiet of his consulting-room ... the psychologist cannot avoid coming to grips with contemporary history, even if his very soul shrinks from the political uproar, the lying propaganda and the jarring speeches of the demagogues (1964).

Conclusion

News is a stressor on the human psyche, not only on vulnerable people like sufferers of PTSD as other studies have found. War journalism—the dominant form of journalism, which sells itself with political spin and the most frightening news of the day—contributes to lingering states like terror, shame and depression. It is a similar psychic mechanism to that triggered by dysfunctional experiences of early childhood.

Existentially, we are frustrated—even angry—that, in the digital age of information overload, we are bombarded with images of war, terrorism and climate change. We feel the "pain" of people and of the planet, but these are hollow feelings. We feel "lost," with nothing to believe in; we switch off and we are disconnected from a meaningful relationship with the wider world. News distorts our fundamental sense of what it means to be human.

The media, like therapy, can adapt to help us to become aware of this: they can equip us with skills to challenge the message, to process, juxtapose and re-combine the representations, and to create new meanings and roles for ourselves as global citizens. Peace journalism, which abounds in cues and clues to equip readers and audiences to negotiate their own readings, can have a therapeutic effect. In Mindell's (2002) words, "If you are passive, relative to the media, you will see it as evil and yourself as good. However if you choose to be active, you can ... create your own story" (186). To do so, in a media-saturated world of information overload, would be to fulfill the aspirations for psychotherapy of its founders—Freud and Jung—and to advance the public service mission of the media.

References

Bagdikian, B. 2000. *The Media Monopoly.* 6th ed. Boston, MC: Beacon Press.

Barrell, J. J., Aanstoos, C., Richards, A., and Arons, M. 1987. Human science research methods. *Journal of Humanistic Psychology*, 27(4), pp. 424-457.

Etherington, K. 2004. *Becoming a Reflexive Researcher: Using ourselves in research.* Jessica Kingsley.

Freud, S. 1953/1975. The claims of psycho-analysis to scientific interest (1913). In: *The Standard Edition of the Complete Psychological Works of Sigmund Freud, Vol. XIII.* London: Hogarth Press.

Galtung, J. (nd). *After Violence: 3R, Reconstruction, Reconciliation, Resolution: Coping With Visible and Invisible Effects of War and Violence.*

Glaser, B., G. and Strauss, A.L. 1967. *The Discovery of Grounded Theory: Strategies for Qualitative Research.* Chicago: Aldine.

Goleman, D. 1996. *Emotional Intelligence.* London: Bloomsbury.

Hall, S. 1997. *Representation and the Media.* Media Education Foundation Transcript. Sourced July 23, 2007 at http://www.mediaed.org/handouts/pdfs/HALL-REPMEDIA.pdf.

Heidegger, M. 1927/1962. *Being and Time.* Oxford: Blackwell. Cited (: 1) in: D. Hiles (2005) *Heuristic Inquiry and Participatory Research.* Unpublished CCPE/MA course notes, 16 September.

Hiles, D. 2002a. *Research Methods in Psychotherapy (2).* Unpublished CCPE/MA Course notes.

Hiles, D. 2002b. *Research Methods in Psychotherapy (3).* Unpublished CCPE/MA Course notes.

Janesick, V. J. 2000. The Choreography of Qualitative Research Design. In: N.K. Denzin & Y.S. Lincoln (eds.) *The Handbook of Qualitative Research.* London: Sage.

Jung, C.G. 1964. Preface to Essays on Contemporary Events [pub. 1946]. In: *Collected Works of C.G. Jung,* Vol. 10. London: Routledge & Kegan Paul.

Kempf, W. 2005. Two experiments focusing on de-escalation oriented coverage of post-war conflicts, *Conflict and Communication Online*, 4(2).

Lederach, J.P., 1997. *Building Peace – sustainable reconciliation in divided societies,* Washington DC: United States Institute of Peace Press.

Lee, S., T. and Maslog, C., C. 2005. War or Peace Journalism in Asia. *Journal of Communication,* vol. 55, no. 2, pp. 311-329.

Lee, S., T., Maslog, C., C. and Kim, H., S. 2006. Asian Conflicts and the Iraq War – a comparative framing analysis. *International Communications Gazette,* vol. 68, no. 5-6, pp. 499-518.

Lynch, J. 2008. The developmentalist and the critical: the emerging divide in journalist training as a form of media development intervention in conflict, *Global Change, Peace and Security* (in press).

Lynch, J., and McGoldrick, A. 2005. *Peace Journalism.* Stroud: Hawthorn Press.

Lynch, J., and McGoldrick, A. 2004. *News from the Holy Land. Theory and Practice of Reporting Conflict: A Peace Journalism Video.* Stroud: Hawthorn Press.

Lule, J. 2001. *Daily News, Eternal Stories: the Mythological Role of Journalism.* New York & London: Guilford Press. Quoted in: A. Scherr (2004) Book Review, *Midwest Quarterly,* Summer 2004, 45(4), pp. 428-431.

Maslow, A. H. 1970. *Motivation and Personality.* 2nd ed. New York: Harper & Row.

May, R. 1991. *The Cry for Myth*. New York: Dell.

Mindell, A. 2002. *The Deep Democracy of Open Forums, Practical Steps to Conflict Prevention and Resolution for the Family, Workplace, and World*. Charlottesville: Hampton Roads.

Moeller, S. 1999. *Compassion Fatigue: How the Media Sell Disease, Famine, War and Death*. New York & London: Routledge.

Seigel, J. E. 2005. *The Idea of the Self: Thought and Experience in Europe since the 17th Century*. Cambridge University Press.

Serlin, I. A. 2006. Psychological Effects of the Virtual Media Coverage of the Iraq War: A Postmodern Humanistic Perspective. In: Kimmel, R. & Stout, C. E. (eds.), *Collateral Damage: the Psychological Consequences of America's War on Terrorism*. Westport, C.T: Praeger, an imprint of Greenwood, pp. 145-163.

Smith, J. A., Jarman, M., and Osborn, M. 1999. Doing Interpretative Phenomenological Analysis. In Murray, M. and Chamberlain, K. (eds.) Qualitative Health Psychology. London: Sage.

Szabo, A., and Hopkinson, K. L. 2007. Negative psychological effects of watching the news in the television: relaxation or another intervention may be needed to buffer them! *International Journal of Behavioral Medicine* 14(2), pp. 47-62.

Toffler, A. 1970. *Future Shock*. New York: Random House.

Active and Passive Peace Journalism in Reporting of the "War on Terrorism" in the Philippines

Jake Lynch

The "War on Terrorism" Ideology

The "7/7" London bombings of July 2005 were interpreted by many in the U.K. as a manifestation of "blowback," "[a] term ... which officials of the [U.S.] Central Intelligence Agency first invented for their own internal use ... refer[ring] to the unintended consequences of [government] policies" (Johnson, 2000, 8). The conservative *Daily Telegraph* newspaper published an opinion poll finding that fully 75 percent of Britons saw the bombings, in which 52 people died on the capital's public transport network, as a response to their country's prominent role in the invasion of two Muslim countries, Afghanistan and Iraq (in Lynch, 2007a, 26).

It was a conversation on which Britain's then prime minister, Tony Blair, the chief architect of these policies, was quick to clamp down. Striding to the Downing Street lectern for a press conference with Hamid Karzai, the visiting Afghan president, he declaimed:

> Let me just make one thing clear in relation to people who say, well, the terrorism here is to do with Iraq, or it is to do with Afghanistan, or other things. Of course these terrorists will use Iraq as an excuse, they will use Afghanistan. September 11 of course happened before both of those things, and then the excuse was American policy, or Israel. They will always have their reasons for acting, but we have got to be really careful of almost giving in to the sort of perverted and twisted logic with which they argue.... There is a kind of insidious way that this is looked at where people say, yes, we entirely abhor the methods of these terrorists, but nonetheless we sort of understand what they are saying about American foreign policy, or Iraq, or Afghanistan or Palestine. No—nothing, but nothing, justifies what they are doing (Blair, 2005).

This, in a nutshell, is the ideology of the so-called "War on Terrorism." Collapsing the distinction between understanding political violence and justifying it is, indeed, a pre-condition of the view that "terrorism" is a phenomenon on which it is possible successfully to wage "war" in the first place. It rests on a connection, rigorously enforced in political discourse in the capitals of protagonist states, between "the way a problem is diagnosed and what can be presented as an appropriate remedy" (Lynch and McGoldrick, 2005). In the words of Richard Perle, a leading neo-conservative who, at the time, occupied an influential position at the Pentagon, "We must decontextualise terror.... [A]ny attempt to discuss the 'roots' of terrorism is an attempt to justify it. It simply needs to be fought and destroyed" (in Hari, 2004). Lynch and McGoldrick add: "Report incidents of political violence without context ... and you are likely to incentivize a 'crackdown,' because someone, somewhere, will assume the public have received, from such reports, an idea that this will form a fitting and effective response" (2005).

This has been the signature propaganda ploy for the "War on Terrorism." As the novelist, Gore Vidal put it, "It is not usual for us to examine why anything happens other than to accuse others of motiveless malignity. 'We are good,' announced a deep thinker on American television, 'they are evil' " (Vidal, 2002). "We," in this context, means both the U.S. and allied countries. "You're either with us, or you're with the terrorists," President George W. Bush intoned, after the attacks of 9-11, and many governments took him at his word. The "War on Terrorism" ideology has been assiduously promulgated around the world, and applied, as a ready-made template, to countless local conflicts involving political violence by non-state actors.

The Philippines

The Philippines is beset by two long-running insurgencies: one by the Moro Islamic Liberation Front, fighting for self-determination for the mainly Muslim Moro people, on the southern island of Mindanao; the other, active across the archipelago, by the New People's Army (NPA), armed wing of the Communist Party of the Philippines (known, between them, as the National Democratic Front, or, often, the CPP/NPA/NDF).

The Moro rebellion was triggered by an infamous act of treachery by the military dictator, Ferdinand Marcos (Vitug and Gloria, 2000), and successive governments took different approaches in dealing with it. The "tough guy" movie-actor-turned-president, Joseph Estrada, ordered his troops into "all-out war." However, he was then deposed, by a non-violent uprising, in January 2001, after revelations of corruption lurid even by local standards. His successor, Gloria Macapagal Arroyo, had been his deputy; under pressure to differentiate her administration, she embraced a policy of "all-out peace."

It meant that, when the stage came to be set for Bush's visit to Manila, in December 2003, it was the other group of rebels, the Communists, who found their way on to the list of global "terror groupings" maintained by the U.S. State Department and into the cross-hairs of a government keen to keep on the right side of its powerful ally. American officials prefer to maintain that, for the Philippines, deciding how to deal with the NPA is "an internal matter. [Ambassador Kristie Kenney] said that Washington is not keen on dipping its hands into internal affairs of other countries," the *Manila Times* reported. However, as the Filipino press also reported at around this time, the U.S. supplied the Armed Forces of the Philippines with a squadron of UH-1H "Huey" helicopters, originally used in Vietnam, for their campaign against the rebels.

It's one of a number of apparent contradictions. Another is that, although the NPA were officially regarded as "terrorists" by the U.S. and the European Union, the Philippines itself had no specific anti-terrorism legislation until July 2007. Suspected activists and sympathizers were either shot, in the wave of mysterious killings that has swept the country during the Arroyo years, or charged with other offences. Yet another anomaly is the wording of the new law itself, and the fact that it was drawn up by legislators representing opposition parties, not the government. Its preamble states:

> The State recognizes that the fight against terrorism requires a comprehensive approach, comprising political, economic, diplomatic, military, and legal means duly taking into account the root causes of terrorism without acknowledging these as justifications for terrorist and/or criminal activities. Such measures shall include conflict management and post-conflict peace-building, addressing the roots of conflict by building state capacity and promoting equitable economic development (Philippines Congress, 2007).

Here, then, was a break, at least in rhetorical terms, with the likes of Blair and Perle; an acknowledgement that political violence is something with root causes, a phenomenon that must be seen in context if it is to be properly understood and effectively countered—indicative of tensions, in the local political domain, over the "war on terrorism" ideology now being imported by the Arroyo administration.

This distinction in the representation of conflict is also the starting point for peace journalism. Its chief characteristic, according to the original table drawn up by Johan Galtung (in Lynch and McGoldrick, 2005), is to portray conflicts as taking place in "open space, open time [with] causes and exits anywhere"; while war journalism, on the other hand, leads or leaves its readers and audiences to conclude that conflict is confined to "closed space, closed time [with] causes and exits in [a single] arena." Shinar draws on the Galtung schema to put forward five headings for operationalizing peace journalism into evaluative criteria for content analysis, the first of which is: "To what extent does journalism explore backgrounds and contexts of conflict formation?" (2007).

Journalism about conflict in the Philippines could therefore be seen as a milieu in which to measure the respective definitional power of these representations of conflict, using the peace journalism model. If peace journalism is practiced, as Lynch and McGoldrick suggest, whenever "editors and reporters make choices, about what to report and how to report it, which create opportunities for society at large to consider and to value non-violent responses to conflict," then—given the connection between diagnosis and remedy—the extent to which background and context are explored, in media reports, could equally indicate the relative political traction of the "War on Terrorism," on the one hand, and approaches based on conflict management, peace-building and equitable economic development, on the other.

This rhetorical disjunction between Washington and Manila is, in turn, symbolic of deeper contradictions. The U.S. bought the Philippines from Spain, for $20 million, in 1898. The Americans fought to suppress the Filipino independence movement, establishing a colonial dominion until formal independence at the end of World War II. Thereafter, the country was seen as a reliable Cold War ally, with a defense pact signed in 1951, shortly after the Chinese Revolution. With the Communist uprising having begun in 1969—just as the war in neighboring Vietnam entered a critical phase—U.S. backing for President Ferdinand Marcos extended without interruption from his period of elected office, through the declaration of martial law, in 1972, and beyond. Marcos was a classic example of "a son-of-a-bitch—but *our* son-of-a-bitch"—a sobriquet first applied to Nicaraguan dictator Anastasio Somoza by President Franklin D. Roosevelt (Zepezauer, 1994).

Resistance to martial law found what Coronel argues was its most significant expression in the media, building on the "legacy of a century-long tradition of a fighting, anti-colonial press" (2000, 149). Through the twentieth century, "clandestinely distributed newspapers helped raise awareness of the evils of nearly 400 years of colonial rule, germinating the idea of an independent Philippine nation" (Ibid.).

Towards the end of the Marcos dictatorship, a new newspaper was founded—the *Philippine Daily Inquirer* or *PDI*—with the explicit aim of hastening its downfall. In the early weeks of 1986, it ran a series of high-profile investigative articles, Coronel relates, exposing "the massive cheating which Marcos had engineered in national elections, provoking widespread anger and stoking discontent." She continues:

> The fall of President Marcos, in February 1986, was not just a sensational story. The local Filipino media played a key role in the political confrontation and—it could be argued—tipped the scales in favour of the pro-democracy movement.... In the last years of the Marcos regime, opposition newspapers reported on anti-government demonstrations, showing Filipinos the extent of the protest movement and emboldening them to organise and participate in mass actions. The coverage of the massive cheating conducted by the government in the February 1986 elections that pitted Marcos against Corazon Aquino stoked the public's ire (Ibid.).

To join these dots—Filipino media in general, and the *PDI* in particular, stand at the head of a rich history of resistance to colonial rule, by the Spanish and then the Americans, and later to an exploitative regime backed by Washington. Local conflicts in the Philippines, particularly the Communist insurgency, had already been inserted into one international context in which the U.S. was itself an avowed protagonist—the Cold War—and were now inserted into another, newer one—the "War on Terrorism." Given its particular ideological construction, compared with the founding principles of peace journalism as discussed above, the extent of peace journalism as practiced by the *PDI* is examined, here, as a qualitative indicator, a social artifact, of the degree of resistance to the 'war on terrorism' in one of its strategic target countries.

First Research Question—How Much "Active" Peace Journalism Does the PDI Do?

Conflict coverage in the *Philippine Daily Inquirer* has already been the subject of two exercises in content analysis, based on operationalizing the peace journalism schema in Lee and Maslog (2005) and Lee et al. (2006). Both these studies use 13 indicators, on the basis of which, the authors say, it is "tempting" to conclude that peace journalism is being practiced to a significant degree. In each study, however, three out of the four *least* prevalent indicators are those *most likely* to denote what they call "a genuine desire ... to promote peace and find solutions." Rather:

> The peace journalism framing is highly dependent on criteria of a less interventionist nature, for example, an avoidance of good/bad labels, a non-partisan approach, a multi-party orientation and an avoidance of emotive language. These four indicators,

although important in the overall scheme of peace journalism … are mere extensions of the objectivity credo: reporting the facts as they are. These indicators do not truly exemplify a strong contributory, proactive role by journalists to seek and offer creative solutions and to pave a way for peace and conflict resolution (Lee et al., 2006).

The sample of local conflict coverage in the *PDI* for each of these studies is taken from reporting of the Moro insurgency from April-June 2000—the "all-out war" period under President Estrada. It also, therefore, predates the "War on Terrorism." In Lee et al. (2006), this is compared with the paper's coverage of the invasion of Iraq, in early 2003. By the time the articles sampled for the present study were published, in 2006, not only had local conflicts in the Philippines become clearly linked with an ideology imported from Washington; the U.S. "brand" had also been tarnished by subsequent events in Iraq, forming a context for conflict reporting now "irreversibly penetrated, even dominated, by the rapid and conspicuous unravelling of key propaganda constructs" from that campaign (Lynch, 2008).

As Lewis remarks, "the very force of institutional power, in fact, creates the conditions for slippage and dissociation" (2005). The first research question for the present study, therefore, is calculated to establish whether, in this new context, reporting of conflict in a newspaper already distinguished as a producer of less interventionist, or "passive" peace journalism, might now manifest a higher proportion of "active" peace journalism. The research design for this study effectively sets a more exacting peace journalism "test" than either of those by Lee and colleagues.

The first evaluative criterion, therefore, is the first in Shinar's list of five: whether there is any exploration of background or context in accounts of political violence or responses to it. The presence (or absence) of such exploration is the key, more than the terms in which it appears. The coverage is analyzed, in other words, in terms of framing, drawing on Entman's helpful definition:

> Analysis of frames illuminates the precise way in which influence over a human consciousness is exerted by the transfer (or communication) of information from one location—such as a speech, utterance, news report, or novel—to that consciousness.... To frame is to select some aspects of a perceived reality and make them more salient in a communicating text, in such a way as to *promote a particular problem definition, causal interpretation, moral evaluation, and/or treatment recommendation* (1993).

The second evaluative criterion is the newspaper's response to propaganda, wherein propaganda is defined as "the deliberate and systematic attempt to shape perceptions, manipulate cognitions and direct behavior to achieve a response that furthers the desired intent of the propagandist" (Jowett and O'Donnell, 1999).

Material for the study all appeared between June 16 and July 15, 2006. The start date saw President Arroyo issue an order to the Armed Forces of the Philippines (AFP) to escalate their action against the NPA, with an additional budget of a billion pesos—a classic "crackdown." The launch of this new policy was marked by an abundance of propaganda, intended to trigger what Ross calls "profound psychological responses that encourage reactive ... nationalistic reporting" (2006). Equipped with Jowett and O'Donnell's definition, propaganda can be conceptualized, then, in Hall's terms (1997) as an attempt to fix and limit meaning, seeking to influence both re-encoding, by journalists, and decoding by readers and audiences.

Eco (1981) draws a distinction between "closed" and "open texts" with the former showing a strong tendency to encourage a particular interpretation, while the latter abound in cues for readers and audiences to develop a critical awareness of built-in interpretations, and equip them to form their own, notably by offering and drawing attention to vantage points from which to inspect propaganda from the outside. Articles scored on this indicator if they contained material likely to open war propaganda to what Hall (1980) calls "negotiated" or "oppositional" readings.

The third evaluative criterion for the study was whether the article in question accorded any visibility to initiatives for conflict management or peace-building, whether by official agency or from civil society. Lederach reflects:

> I have not experienced any situation of conflict, no matter how protracted or severe, from Central America to the Philippines to the Horn of Africa, where there have not been people who had a vision for peace, emerging often from their own experience of pain. Far too often, however, these same people are overlooked and disempowered either because they do not represent "official" power, whether on the side of government or the various militias, or because they are written off as biased and too personally affected by the conflict (1997).

Peace journalism began as a project to apply, to media representations, evidence about conflict and peace gleaned by researchers in the field of peace and conflict studies, with Lederach as one of its chief exponents. (Hence Shinar's third criterion: "Does journalism offer creative ideas for conflict resolution, development, peacemaking and peacekeeping?") Where journalism fails to match that evidence, it can be said to be inaccurate: "Good journalism is not a description of the current state of conflict coverage," Kempf remarks (2007). Visions for peace are always there to find, according to Lederach, if we look hard enough; their inclusion, in media representations, is clearly ideational, in this context, because they represent a remedy that corresponds with a diagnosis of the problem of political violence that differs from that offered by the "War on Terrorism" ideology. In simple terms, if peace-building is to be relevant in any discussion of terrorism, then the latter must be allowed to be "about" something—to arise in a context, to germinate in identifiable conditions which can be alleviated and removed.

Results

Articles for the study were retrieved from the *Philippine Daily Inquirer*'s own website. They had all been first published in the newspaper itself. In the table below, the notation, "WJ" indicates articles with none of the three indicators present. "PJ" articles showed at least one of the three indicators; in some cases, more than one. The percentage of PJ therefore refers to articles with at least some active peace journalism, as a proportion of the overall number of articles in the sample.

Another way of putting the results, therefore, would be to say that, in 85 articles in the *PDI*, active peace journalism indicators occurred 50 times in 35 of the articles. In the two previous studies, the numerical results given for the occurrence of particular peace journalism indicators are not broken down per publication, but are given, instead, across the whole sample—consisting of the *PDI* and nine other newspapers from five Asian countries, in the case of Lee and Maslog (2005), and seven others from the same five countries, in Lee et al. (2006). Of their criteria, two most closely match the ones applied here. Where I have counted the number of articles exploring contexts and backgrounds, they use the notation, "causes and consequences," which crop up in 6.0 percent of the articles in the earlier study, and 5.5 percent in the later one. Where I have counted articles that make peace visible, by picking up, and retailing, as it were, into the public sphere, calls, plans and suggestions for non-violent conflict responses, they use the notation, "proactive," which is found in just 3.7 percent of the first sample and 3.0 percent of the second.[1] In this study, peace is made visible in 16.4 percent, while backgrounds and contexts are explored in 21.2 percent of *PDI* articles.

Neither of the previous two studies includes any indicator for propaganda. The Galtung table contained four quadrants for each of the two forms, war journalism and peace journalism. Where the former was orientated towards violence, towards propaganda, towards elites and towards victory, the latter was peace-orientated, truth-orientated, people-orientated and solution-orientated. The indicators used by Lee and colleagues cover all except the issue of propaganda, on the war journalism side, and, in peace journalism, measures to counter it. As discussed earlier, such measures are construed here as being more elaborate than simply "truth." As I note in an earlier work:

> There is no dispute over a journalist's duty to truthfulness.... Reporters should report, as accurately and fully as they can, the facts they encounter. Where peace journalism goes further is to call on them to consider how and why these particular facts, as distinct from a practically infinite number of others "out there," come to meet them; and how they, the reporters, come to meet these particular facts (Lynch, 2007b).

These are also some of the first questions the reader needs to consider in order to negotiate his or her own reading of a heavily encoded discourse such as news journalism—especially when, influenced by war propaganda, it does ideological work by, as Hall puts it, "naturalis[ing] representation to the point where you cannot see that anyone produced it" (1997). The proportion of *PDI* articles that discuss how and why the constructs of propaganda, familiar from the "War on Terrorism" ideology, are now being applied to local conflicts—and/or explicitly take issue with them—is 23.5 percent.

Second Research Question: How Much "Passive" Peace Journalism Does the PDI Do?

Most of the high ratings for newspapers in the studies by Lee and colleagues are accounted for by the presence of three indicators of "passive" peace journalism:

- Avoiding emotive or demonizing language;
- Non-partisan coverage; and
- Avoiding labeling as "good or bad."

Table 1
Numerical results from the *Philippine Daily Inquirer*

	Number of articles	WJ	PJ	Percentage of PJ	Explore Context	Challenge Propaganda	Make Peace Visible
Communist insurgency	64	37	27	42.2%	14	15	11
Moro insurgency	21	13	8	38.1%	4	5	3
Total	85	50	35	41.2%	18	20	14

Once again, the figures are not broken down per publication, so it is possible only to deduce the *PDI* performance on these criteria. In Lee and Maslog (2005), the paper scored an overall 59.0 percent of peace journalism compared with 35.7 percent for the whole sample, a multiplier of 1.65. In Lee et al. (2006), the *PDI* registered 63.2 percent against an overall total of 41.1 percent, a multiplier of 1.54, giving an average "*PDI* peace journalism premium" of 1.595. Using this as a multiplier of the average results for each of the three passive peace journalism indicators, one can deduce a *PDI* score, for comparison with the findings on the same criteria from the present study, in Table 2.

In neither of the earlier studies do the authors offer a detailed description, illustrated with examples, of how these criteria are applied. For the present study, in order to avoid giving an inflated score, attempts have been made to apply the criteria stringently, so articles failed to register on these indicators if they contained even a slight trace of emotive or demonizing language, partisanship or labeling as "good and bad."

In one interesting example, an article about the Moro insurgency contained the phrase, "Muslim commanders." A reference apparently innocuous to the outside observer, especially as the main insurgent group actually calls itself the Moro *Islamic* Liberation Front (emphasis added). The practice of appending the word "Muslim" in this way has been called into controversy in the Philippines, to the point where senior journalists were summoned to appear before Senate committees considering draft legislation to ban it. Introduced in 2000, the bill called for the "prohibit[ion of] the use of the word 'Muslim' in print or broadcast media" except in non-pejorative contexts. It failed for lack of time, but the initiative both reflected and reinforced widespread awareness of the issue in political and media circles.

Table 2
***PDI* scores across studies.**

Indicator	PDI score deduced from earlier studies	PDI score from this study
Avoiding emotive or demonizing language	24.0%	40.0%
Non-partisan	21.9%	49.4%
Avoiding labeling as "good and bad"	16.9%	64.7%

Third Research Question: How Does the PDI Compare with
International Media?

The *PDI*'s prowess is well established—on indicators of both passive and now active peace journalism. In Lee et al. (2006) it even bucks the general trend, that the newspapers under examination were more inclined to produce peace journalism in coverage of the Iraq war than of local conflicts; albeit the difference is very small. However, the study does not peer through that telescope from the other end, as it were. It looks at local coverage of both an international and a local conflict, but does not compare international coverage of the local conflict in any given case.

President Arroyo's *demarche* of June 2006 was sufficient to trigger significant interest among international media. The general research background indicates that their coverage "should" prove more likely to avoid partisanship, demonizing language and so forth, scoring highly—at least on passive peace journalism indicators—relative to local media. Nossek, for instance, sets out to examine the well-known alignment of news with nation and test how far it still applies even after "the accelerated technological development of 1990s, which left its mark on the communication map" (2004). Looking specifically at representations of political violence, or "terrorism," he finds, "When a foreign news item is defined as "ours," then journalists' professional practices become subordinate to national loyalty; when an item is "theirs," journalistic professionalism comes into its own" (Ibid.).

Nossek bases his definition of "professional" journalistic practices on Roeh and Cohen's research on the "openness" and "closedness" of television news items, to include such factors as balance, neutrality, and the drawing of clear distinction between fact and commentary (2004). There is, in other words, a substantial overlap, both with Eco's concept of open and closed texts and with formulations of journalism's public service role such as the highly influential BBC *Editorial Guidelines*, with their call for program-makers to enable audiences to "form their own views" by "support[ing] fair and informed debate" (BBC, 2007).

Lynch and McGoldrick have argued that the conventions of war jour-nalism, where they prevail, are inimical to delivering on this promise, especially as the same document explains how this aim is to be achieved. Its provisions include the following: "We strive to reflect a wide range of opinion and explore a range and conflict of views so that no significant strand of thought is knowingly unreflected or under-represented." Peace journalism, with its call to broaden the range of sources for news so as to "make audible and visible the subjugated aspects of reality" (Galtung, in Lynch and McGoldrick, 2005)—including those, in Lederach's terms, overlooked, disempowered, or written off by official political discourses—makes such inclusiveness an indispensable aspect of the journalist's professional repertoire.

In so far as peace journalism is needed for editors and reporters to deliver on their public service remit, especially in providing texts sufficiently open for audiences (and readers) to form their own views—to decode propaganda, indeed—Nossek's criteria of professionalism could be read as a rough equivalent of peace journalism. What he characterizes as a "theoretical assumption ... that the more 'national' the report is, the less 'professional' it will be (i.e., the closer the reporters/editors to a given news event in terms of national interest), the further they are from applying professional news values" is indeed borne out by his study, even in today's globalized conditions.

So how does coverage in international media in this period compare with that in the *PDI*? Articles from the same date range were harvested from the Factiva professional search engine, with an initial search for any item containing the term, "Philippines." Articles reproduced from Philippines newspapers themselves were first weeded out, along with any repeats. Then the sample was further winnowed down, purposively, to form a set of articles dealing explicitly with either of the two insurgencies. For the most part, the remaining items were from major international and regional agencies with their own Manila bureau—Reuters, Xinhua, Agence France Presse, Gulf News, Thai News Service, Asia Pulse, and the like. There was the occasional contribution from reporters commissioned by individual newspapers, among them, publications in the U.S., New Zealand, and the U.K.

Comparing these results with those from the *PDI* shows how that paper confutes the general pattern hypothesized, then tested and broadly confirmed, by Nossek, albeit in different contexts. There is less peace journalism, whether passive or active, on every indicator, in international media than there is in the *PDI*.

Some of this distinction may be accounted for by a factor also mentioned in Lee et al. (2006), namely that copy from foreign wire services, prominently represented in the sample of international media, tends to consist of concise daily updates rather than more in-depth feature articles with commensurately greater scope for the inclusion of contextualizing material.

Table 3
Numerical results from international media.

	Communist insurgency	Moro insurgency	Overall
Total number of articles	222	61	283
WJ	163	47	210
PJ	59	14	73
Explore context	34	11	45
Challenge Propaganda	15	1	16
Make peace visible	17	7	24
Percentage of "active peace journalism"	26.6%	22.9%	25.8%
Avoid emotive/demonizing language	15.3%	18.0%	15.9%
Non-partisan	26.1%	24.5%	25.8%
Avoid labeling as "good and bad"	31.5%	31.1%	31.4%

The sheer length of the stories in the respective samples is significant in this respect—the mean average number of paragraphs in the *PDI* articles was 11.2, whereas in the articles from international media it was 9.5.

However, the findings also reflect the difference in willingness to accept and reproduce key propaganda constructs. In the 283 articles in the international media sample, for instance, fully 133 (47 percent) mention either the word "terror", or "terrorist" or "terrorism" or a combination of two or more. In the *PDI* articles, the incidence is much less, appearing in just 18 out of 85 articles, or 21.2 percent. In the case of articles about the Communist insurgency, most of these take the form of simple reminders to readers that the breakdown in the peace process between the NPA and the Philippines government came when the former was placed on the U.S. and E.U. lists of "terrorist organizations."

The Texts

One example of a text containing more than one characteristic of peace journalism is among several in the *PDI* that take issue with propaganda around the proposition that the Communist insurgency should, or indeed can, be ended by violent means. Headed, "A bloodless way to end communist rebellion," an opinion piece from near the end of the study period reminds readers that the Arroyo government, in declaring all-out war against the NPA, was following the lead of "every other administration in the past"—the implication being, clearly that such an approach was doomed to fail.

Instead, the remedy, the writer contended, was "to seriously implement genuine agrarian reform [to] free poor farmers from the oppressive and exploitative shackles of landlords and traders." At the moment, it explained, the proceeds from their produce went largely to "landowners and the manipulative traders and usurers," making the NPA's message of "agrarian revolution" seem attractive. Reform agriculture so as to let them control more of their own production and its appeal will diminish. "Nationalist industrialization"—diversifying the Philippines' industrial base so as to provide jobs and development—and the elimination of corruption, were the other two parts of the writer's suggested strategy for tackling the insurgency. This article was classified, in the study, as exhibiting all three active peace journalism characteristics.

A couple of weeks after the AFP received their new orders, indeed, the *Inquirer* declared, in an editorial, its own skepticism of the strategy, "We cannot send our soldiers to battle an endless insurgency.... [H]istory tells us an all-out war on a guerrilla movement cannot be won." A "realistic strategy," the paper continued, would include, "forc[ing] the insurgents off the battlefield and on to the negotiating table.... [It] also requires draining the water in which the fishes swim; that is, convincing the population in a communist area of influence of the alternatives, and providing public services even in the remotest *barrio*."

Another editorial picked up on the ominous statement by Justice Secretary Raul Gonzalez that the campaign against the NPA would inevitably inflict "collateral damage." A subsequent opinion article, by an officer of the Centre for Trade Union and Human Rights (CTUHR), linked this with the ongoing wave of mysterious killings in the Philippines, with well-attested suspicions of AFP involvement. "CTUHR documentation shows that those who have been killed and are continuously being harassed ... belong to legitimate unions and organizations. They are ordinary workers who only ask for fair wages, decent jobs or a venue where they can air their concerns." "As long as people are mired in poverty and victimized by social injustice," it continued, "there will always be critics and insurgents."

In government statements reported in the latter part of the study period, it was not unusual to see officials draw attention to portions of the billion-peso "fighting fund," set aside by Arroyo to defeat the insurgency, earmarked for measures to reduce poverty in communist areas of influence. This did not, of itself, qualify the articles in question as examples of peace journalism. The aim of reducing poverty is, notionally at least, widely shared. It's nearly a decade now since the International Monetary Fund renamed its "Enhanced Structural Adjustment Facility" as the "Poverty Reduction and Growth Facility," though one critic at the time observed, "When the IMF speaks of poverty relief it's like telling someone who is beating their wife, 'We're going to provide transport for your wife to the hospital' " (Aslam, 1999).

In Washington, meanwhile, by September 2002, those in charge of drafting a speech for President Bush to launch the new U.S. National Security Strategy saw fit to include the following passage: "Poverty does not make poor people into terrorists and murderers. Yet poverty, weak institutions, and corruption can make weak states vulnerable to terrorist networks and drug cartels within their borders" (Bush, 2002).

Notwithstanding the more extreme versions of "War on Terrorism" ideology—such as those furnished by Perle and Blair—there was, from its early stages, at least some rhetorical acknowledgement of poverty as a driver of political violence. But "poverty," by itself, is too simplistic to fulfill, simply by being invoked, Shinar's first test of exploring the backgrounds and contexts of conflict formation. To qualify as peace journalism on this count, an article in the study had to include some allusion to the concept named by Gurr, in a landmark text, as "relative deprivation," identified as the prime cause of human aggression and the main reason "why men rebel." Relative deprivation is defined as "the discrepancy between what people think they deserve, and what they think they can get.... The potential for collective violence varies strongly with the intensity and scope of relative deprivation among members of a collectivity" (1970).

Hence, the article quoted earlier, with its reference to social injustice, "counted"; as did another column in which the connections were further spelt out, "Felt injustice and human rights violations that accompany militarization and development projects appear more directly to push people to take up arms." The reference to development projects emphasizes the distinction here—many initiatives labeled as ways to "reduce poverty," such as parceling up land and granting farming or mining concessions on it to international business, can prove divisive and actually increase relative deprivation for substantial sections of the population (Nettleton et al., nd). (Hence, perhaps, the reference in the anti-terrorism legislation to "*equitable* economic development"—emphasis added).

Conclusion

The *Philippines Daily Inquirer* is a notable purveyor of peace journalism, measured on both passive and active indicators. This applies even in a phase where the government of its own country of origin is engaged in a concerted intensification of a major internal conflict. Coverage in the *PDI* of the Philippines' two long-running insurgencies still scores considerably higher, in this phase, than reporting of the same conflicts in international media on a range of evaluative criteria developed from the peace journalism schema.

Moreover, the peace journalism performance of the *PDI* has increased markedly since the declaration of the "War on Terrorism" and its imbrication into at least one of these two internal conflicts, against the communist New People's Army. The "War on Terrorism" ideology has been assiduously promoted from Washington and exported to allied countries such as the Philippines, but that process has generated its own resistance, in the news domain as in others. In McNair's words:

> While the desire for control of the news agenda, and for definitional power in the journalistic construction of meaning, are powerful and ever-present, not least in a time of war and perceived global crisis, the capacity of elite groups to wield it effectively is more limited than it has been since the emergence of the first news media in the sixteenth century (2006).

The journalistic field, to use Bourdieu's term, is "a relatively autonomous institutional sphere, one which articulates with relations of power, knowledge and production more broadly, but which also has a certain logic of its own" (1999). The field of Filipino media, exemplified by the *PDI*, articulates, in turn, with a larger struggle for definitional power and dominance in its own region.

The fall of Marcos in 1986 could be seen as the last of a notable series of reverses for U.S. interests around the world during the crisis of military legitimacy following Vietnam, also including points as far apart as Nicaragua (the Somozas' overthrow), Mozambique, and Iran (Lynch, 2007c). The new Philippines Congress marked the break with the past by outlawing the siting of foreign military installations on its soil. Clark Air Base and U.S. Naval Base Subic Bay, anchors and symbols of U.S. power, were duly closed.

The country's strategic significance remains evident, however, especially in today's context of a struggle for influence over Southeast Asia between exponents of the "Washington Consensus" and an emerging "Beijing Consensus" (Desker, 2007). The monitoring group, Focus on the Global South, reported in 2007 that the increasing presence of visiting U.S. troops in the southern Philippines, under the rubric of cooperation in the "War on Terrorism," was in fact a cover for the surreptitious re-establishment of *de facto* military bases as a strategic asset in the larger struggle with China. The "Revolution in Military Affairs" of the present century now meant that such installations could be much smaller than in previous eras, the report pointed out, and still fulfill a strategic role; within areas set aside for the Armed Forces of the Philippines, so-called U.S. "lily pads" were now taking root (Focus, 2007).

So, struggles over the definition and representation of conflict in the Philippines, as manifest in journalistic responses to attempts to import or export the "War on Terrorism" ideology and apply it to political violence associated with the two insurgencies, could be construed as a social artifact of a wider conflict involving rival projects to exert hegemonic power in East Asia, identified by the Pentagon as one of three key areas of contestation for global influence, along with Europe and the Middle East, in the post-Cold War policy document, *Defense Planning Guidance*, by Paul Wolfowitz, Zalmay Khalilzad, and Lewis Libby (in Tyler, 1992).

The NPA espouse the doctrines of Chairman Mao, in particular the concept of "People's War" as their inspiration. To promote non-violent responses to conflict, as contributors to the *PDI* themselves opined, will require underlying issues to be addressed—almost certainly including arrangements for a more equitable distribution of the fruits of agricultural labor, an industrial strategy for sustainable national development and the elimination of corruption. It would also require measures to tackle another of the *PDI*'s preoccupations through this period—the abuse of human rights as manifest in the hundreds of mysterious killings of left-wing activists under the administration of Gloria Arroyo.

To pick up calls for, and articulations of such policies, from whatever quarter and remit them into the public sphere is one contribution journalists can make to peace and to preventing people's aspirations for betterment from falling victim to geo-strategic rivalries and their attendant ideological constructs. A notable public service, indeed, and, to use the words of Lee et al., "a strong, contributory, proactive role." It is a role the *PDI* is playing, on the basis of findings from this and two other studies, and it sets an example for others to follow.

Note

1.   In quoting figures from Lee et al. (2006), I am using only those from the articles pertaining to local conflicts, not the Iraq war.

References

Aslam, Abid. 1999. *IMF's new poverty focus a hard sell*, Interpress Service, retrieved January 4, 2008 from http://www.twnside.org.sg/title/sell-cn.htm.

BBC. 2007. *Editorial Guidelines*, retrieved August 24 2007 from http://www.bbc.co.uk/guidelines/editorialguidelines/edguide/impartiality/.

Blair, Tony. 2005. Downing Street news conference, transcript retrieved December 18, 2007 http://www.number10.gov.uk/output/Page7955.asp.

Bourdieu, Pierre. 1999. *On Television* (trans. Priscilla Parkhurst Ferguson), New York: New Press.

Bush, George, W. 2002. National Security Strategy of the United States, retrieved December 18, 2007 from http://www.whitehouse.gov/nsc/nssall.html.

Coronel, Sheila, S. 2000. "Free as a mocking bird," in Louise Williams and Roland Rich (eds.), *Losing Control—Freedom of the Press in Asia*, Canberra: Asia Pacific Press, pp. 147-168.

Desker, Barry. 2007. *New Security Dimensions in the Asia-Pacific*, Michael Hintze Inaugural Lecture, Centre for International Security Studies, University of Sydney. Text can be downloaded from http://ciss.econ.usyd.edu.au/events/.

Eco, Umberto. 1992. *The Role of the Reader*, London, Hutchinson.

Entman, Robert. 1993. "Framing: Towards Clarification of a Fractured Paradigm," *Journal of Communication*, vol. 43, pp. 51-8.

Focus. 2007. "An acceptable pattern of deployment," Focus on the Global South, Focusweb, November 24.

Gurr, E. R. 1970. *Why Men Rebel*, Princeton, NJ: Princeton University Press.

Hall, Stuart. 1980. "Encoding/Decoding," in *Culture, Media, Language: working papers in cultural studies*, 1972-79, (ed) S. Hall et al., London: Hutchinson, pp .128-138.

Hall, Stuart, 1997. *Representation and the Media*. Media Education Foundation Transcript, retrieved 23 July 2007 from http://www.mediaed.org/handouts/pdfs/HALL-REPMEDIA.pdf.

Hari, Johann, 2004. "The 'War on Terror' is way off course," *Independent*, September 22.

Johnson, Chalmers, 2000. *Blowback: the costs and consequences of American Empire*, New York: Metropolitan Books.

Jowett, Garth, S., and O'Donnell, Victoria. 1999. *Power and Persuasion*, London: Sage.

Kempf, Wilhelm, 2007. "Peace journalism: a tightrope walk between advocacy journalism and constructive conflict coverage," *Conflict and Communication Online*, 6(2).

Lederach, John Paul, 1997. *Building Peace—sustainable reconciliation in divided societies*, Washington DC: United States Institute of Peace Press.

Lee, S.T., and Maslog, C.C. 2005. "War or Peace Journalism in Asia," *Journal of Communication*, 55(2), pp. 311-329.

Lee, S.T., Maslog, C.C., and Kim, H.S. 2006. Asian Conflicts and the Iraq War—a comparative framing analysis. *International Communications Gazette*, 68(5-6), pp. 499-518.

Lewis, Jeff. 2005. *Language Wars—the role of media and culture in global terror and political violence*, London: Pluto Press.

Lynch, Jake. 2007a. "Issues in the media coverage of terrorism," *Media Development*, World Association for Christian Communication, Vol. LIV, 3/2007, pp. 22-27.

Lynch, Jake. 2007b. "Peace Journalism and its discontents," *Conflict and Communication Online*, 6(2).

Lynch, Jake. 2007c. Promoting *Dissent, Reviving Democracy*. Sydney Peace Foundation Tenth Anniversary Lecture, Occasional Paper 2007/1, CPACS, University of Sydney.

Lynch, Jake. 2008. "The Peace Journalism condition—conflict reporting for the post-aligned mediascape," in Galtung, Johan and Lynch, Jake, *New Directions in Peace Journalism*, Boulder: Paradigm Press (in press).

Lynch, Jake and McGoldrick, Annabel. 2005. *Peace Journalism*, Stroud: Hawthorn Press.

McNair, Brian. 2006. *Cultural chaos—journalism, news and power in a globalised world*, Oxford: Routledge.

Nettleton, Geoff, Whitmore, Andy and Glennie, Jonathan, nd. *Breaking promises, making profits: mining in The Philippines*, London: Christian Aid and Philippines Indigenous People's Links.

Nossek, Hillel. 2004. "Our News and their News," *Journalism*, 5(3), pp. 343-368.

Philippines Congress. 2007. Republic Act No. 9372—An act to secure the state and protect our people from terrorism.

Ross, Susan, Dente. 2006. [De]Constructing Conflict: A Focused Review of War and Peace Journalism, *Conflict and Communication Online*, 5(2), pp. 1-19.

Ross, Susan, Dente. 2007. Peace Journalism: Constructive Media in a Global Community, *Global Media Journal (Mediterranean Edition)*, 2(2), pp. 77-81.

Shinar, Dov. 2007. "Peace Journalism—The State of the Art," in *Peace Journalism —The State of the Art*, Dov Shinar and Wilhelm Kempf (eds.), pp. 199-210. Berlin: Regener.

Tyler, Patrick, E. 1992. U.S. Strategy Plan Calls for Insuring No Rivals Develop A One-Superpower World, *New York Times*, March 8.

Vidal, Gore. 2002. "Taking Liberties," *Guardian*, April 27, online version retrieved December 18, 2007 from http://www.guardian.co.uk/afghanistan/comment/story/0,11447,698584,00.html.

Vitug, Marites, D., and Gloria, Glenda, M. 2000. *Under the Crescent Moon: Rebellion in Mindanao*, Manila: Ateneo Center for Social Policy and Public Affairs/Institute for Popular Democracy.

Zepezauer, Mark. 1994. *The CIA's Greatest Hits*, Boston: Odonian Press.

Peace, Conflict, and Communication: A Focused Bibliography of Recent Contributions

Susan Dente Ross

Annabring, U., Ditlmann, R., and Kempf, W. 2005. Die kognitive Repräsentation von Nachkriegskonflikten im Spannungsfeld zwischen Mainstream-Diskurs und abweichender Berichterstattung. In Projektgruppe Friedensforschung Konstanz (Hrsg.), *Nachrichtenmedien als Mediatoren von Peace-Building, Demokratisierung und Versöhnung in Nachkriegsgesellschaften,* pp. 235-254. Berlin: Regener.

Bishop, J., J. Kang-Graham, J. Hmielowski, A. Morozov, B. White and S. D. Ross. 2007. Discourses of Blame and Responsibility: U.S./Canadian Media Representations of Palestinian/Israeli Relations, *Conflict & Communication,* 6(1), April.

Bläsi, B., Jaeger, S., Kempf, W., Kondopoulou, M., and Paskoski, D. 2005. Konstruktive Aspekte des serbischen, deutschen und griechischen Nachkriegsdiskurses—qualitative Vergleichsstudien. In Projektgruppe Friedensforschung Konstanz (Hrsg.), *Nachrichtenmedien als Mediatoren von Peace-Building, Demokratisierung und Versöhnung in Nachkriegsgesellschaften,* pp. 149-200. Berlin: Regener.

Bläsi, B., Jaeger, S., Kempf, W., and Spohrs, M. 2005. Glaubwürdigkeit und Attraktivität von eskalations- und deeskalationsorientierten Nachrichtentexten. In Projektgruppe Friedensforschung Konstanz (Hrsg.), *Nachrichtenmedien als Mediatoren von Peace-Building, Demokratisierung und Versöhnung in Nachkriegsgesellschaften.* Berlin: Regener.

Hackett, R. A. 2002. Covering up the "War on Terrorism": The Master Frame and the Media Chill. In Peter Phillips & Project Censored, *Censored 2003: The Top 25 Censored Stories,* pp. 131-38. New York: Seven Stories Press.

Hackett, R. A. 2004. Drumbeating for war? Media versus peace and democracy. In George Melnyk (ed.), *Canada and the New American Empire,* 171-81. University of Calgary Press.

Hackett, R. A. 2006. "Is peace journalism possible? Three frameworks for analyzing structure and agency in news media," *Conflict & Communication,* 4(2) (October). Republished (2007) in Dov Shinar and Wilhelm Kempf (eds.), *Peace Journalism: The State of the Art,* pp. 75-94. Berlin: Regener.

Hackett, R. A. 2007. "Journalism versus peace? Notes on a problematic relationship," *Global Media Journal, Mediterranean Edition,* 2(1), Spring, pp. 47-53.

Hackett, R. A., and Carroll, W. K. 2006. *Remaking Media: The struggle to democratize public communication.* London: Routledge.

Hackett, R. A., and Zhao, Y. (eds.) 2005. *Democratizing Global Media: One world, many struggles.* Boulder, CO: Rowman & Littlefield with the Toda Institute for Global Peace and Policy Research.

Jaeger, S., and Kempf, W. 2005. Möglichkeiten und Grenzen konstruktiver Nachkriegs-berichterstattung. In Projektgruppe Friedensforschung Konstanz (Hrsg.), *Nachrichtenmedien als Mediatoren von Peace-Building, Demokratisierung und Versöhnung in Nachkriegsgesellschaften*, pp. 277-285. Berlin: Regener.

Jaeger, S., and Kempf, W. 2003. Ursachen und Entwicklungsperspektiven von Konflikt und Gewalt. Perspektiven für eine europäische Friedenspolitik. In Eberwein, W.-D. (Koord.), *Europäische Friedenspolitik – Politik einer Friedensmacht?*, pp. 68-88. Münster: Agenda.

Jaeger, S., and Kempf, W. 2005. Von der Theorie zur Empirie. In Projektgruppe Friedensforschung Konstanz (Hrsg.), *Nachrichtenmedien als Mediatoren von Peace-Building, Demokratisierung und Versöhnung in Nachkriegsgesellschaften*, pp. 36-50. Berlin: Regener.

Kempf, W. 2003. Constructive conflict coverage—A social-psychological research and development program (Also Konstruktive Konfliktberichterstattung—Ein sozialpsychologisches Forschungs—und Entwicklungsprogramm), *Conflict & Communication*, 2(2). Republished and edited by the Austrian Study Centre for Peace and Conflict Resolution (ASPR). Berlin: Regener. (190S.)

Kempf, W. 2007. Die Projektgruppe Friedensforschung Konstanz, *Wissenschaft & Frieden*, 25(3), pp. 32-33.

Kempf, W. (2003, 2006 2nd). *Forschungsmethoden der Psychologie. Zwischen naturwissenschaftlichem Experiment und sozialwissenschaftlicher Hermeneutik. Band I: Theorie und Empire*. Berlin: Regener. (368S.). Zweite überarbeitete und erweiterte Auflage (377S.)

Kempf, W. 2004. Friedensjournalismus. In Sommer, G. and Fuchs, A. (Eds.), *Krieg und Frieden. Handbuch der Konflikt- und Friedenspsychologie*, pp. 439-451. Stuttgart: Beltz-PVU.

Kempf, W. 2005. Modelle des Friedensjournalismus. In Projektgruppe Friedensforschung Konstanz (Hrsg.), *Nachrichtenmedien als Mediatoren von Peace-Building, Demokratisierung und Versöhnung in Nachkriegsgesellschaften*, pp. 13-35. Berlin: Regener.

Kempf, W. 2007. Peace Journalism: A tightrope walk between advocacy journalism and constructive conflict coverage, *Conflict & Communication*, 6(2).

Kempf, W. 2006. September 11 and the Need for a Social Science Research Agenda. In Peleg, S. and Kempf, W. (eds.), *Fighting Terrorism in the Liberal State: An Integrated Model of Research, Intelligence and International Law*, pp. 14-19. Amsterdam: IOS-Press.

Kempf, W. 2006. Social constructivism and its implications for critical media studies, *Conflict & Communication*, 5(1).

Kempf, W. 2005. Two experiments focusing on de-escalation oriented coverage of postwar conflicts, *Conflict & Communication*, 4(2). Republished (2007) in Dov Shinar and Wilhelm Kempf (eds.), *Peace Journalism: The State of the Art*. Berlin: Regener.

Kempf, W., Brice, J., Schulz, C.A., and Reimann, M. 2007. Introduction to constructive conflict coverage—An eLearning module, *Diskussionsbeiträge der Projektgruppe Friedensforschung Konstanz*. No. 61/2007.

Lynch, J. 2007. A course in Peace Journalism. In Dov Shinar and Wilhelm Kempf (eds.), *Peace Journalism: The State of the Art*. Berlin: Regener Publishing.

Lynch, J. 2007. A reply to the replies, *Conflict & Communication*, 6(2).

Lynch, J. 2007. Peace Journalism and its discontents, *Conflict & Communication*, 6(2).

Lynch, J. 2004. Reporting Iraq—What went right? What went wrong? *Mediactive*, 3, Mediawar. London: Barefoot Publications.

Lynch, J. 2002. *Reporting the World*. Taplow, U.K.: Conflict & Peace Forums.

Lynch, J. 2004. Reporting the World. In Chris Paterson and Annabelle Sreberny (eds.), *International News in the 21st Century*. Eastleigh, U.K.: John Libbey.

Lynch, J. 2004. Reporting the World: An ethical challenge to international news. In M. Caparini (ed.), *Media in Security and Governance*. Baden-Baden: Nomos Verlagsgesellschaft.

Lynch, J. 2006. What's so great about Peace Journalism? *Global Media Journal: Mediterranean Edition*, 1(1).

Lynch, J., and Galtung, J. 2008. *Reporting Conflict—An introduction to Peace Journalism*. Boulder, CO: Paradigm Press.

Lynch, J., and McGoldrick, A. 2004. *News from the Holy Land* (50 mins with 40pp teaching notes). Princeton, NJ: Hawthorn Press, Stroud, and Films for the Humanities and Sciences.

Lynch, J., and McGoldrick, A. 2005. *Peace Journalism*. Stroud, U.K.: Hawthorn Press.

Lynch, J., and McGoldrick, A. 2007. Peace Journalism. In C. Webel and J. Galtung (eds), *Handbook of Peace and Conflict Studies*. Abingdon, U.K.: Routledge.

Lynch, J., and McGoldrick, A. 2005. Peace Journalism—A global dialog for democracy and democratic media. In R.A. Hackett and Y. Zhao (eds.), *Democratizing Global Media*. Lanham, CO: Rowman.

Lynch, J., and McGoldrick, A. 2004. Peace Journalism in Indonesia. In Thomas Hanitzsch, Martin Loffelholz and Ronny Mustamu (Eds.), *Agents of Peace: Public Communication and Conflict Resolution in an Asian Setting*. Jakarta: Friedrich Ebert Stiftung.

Lynch, J., and McGoldrick, A. 2007. *Peace Journalism in the Philippines* (40 mins). University of Sydney: Centre for Peace and Conflict Studies.

Lynch, J., and McGoldrick, A. 2003. Tips for Covering Conflict. In Danny Schechter (ed), *Media Wars: News at a time of terror*. Lanham, U.K.: Rowman and Littlefield.

Mandelzis, L. 2007. Representation of peace in news discourse: Viewpoint and opportunity for peace journalism. In D. Shinar and W. Kempf (eds.), *Peace Journalism: The State of the Art*. Berlin: Regener.

Mandelzis, L. 2003. The Changing Image of the Enemy in the Israeli News Discourse, *conflict & communication*, 2(1).

Mandelzis, L. 2007. Representations of Peace in News Discourse: Viewpoint and Opportunity for Peace Journalism, *Conflict & Communication*, 6(1).

Mandelzis, L., and Naveh, C. 2006. American Crisis—Israeli Narrative: The Role of the Media Discourse in the Promotion of a War Agenda. In Nikolaev, A.G. and E.A Hakanen (Eds.), *Leading to the 2003 Iraq War: The Global Media Debate*. New York: Palgrave Macmillan.

McGoldrick, A. 2007. War journalism and "objectivity." In Dov Shinar and Wilhelm Kempf (eds), *Peace Journalism: The State of the Art*. Berlin: Regener Publishing.

Ottosen, R. 2007. Emphasizing Images in Peace Journalism: Theory and Practice in the Case of Norway's Biggest Newspaper, *Conflict & Communication*, 2.

Ottosen, R. 2004. *Fiction or News? A Quest for Multidisciplinary Research on the Entertainment Industry and Its Effects on Journalism*. Nordicom Information No. 2.

Ottosen, R. 2005. Good-doers or Bad-doers? Images of the War in Iraq in the Mainstream Norwegian Press. In Ottosen, Rune and Nohrstedt, Stig A (eds.), *Global War – Local Views. Media Images of the Iraq War*. Gothenburg: Nordicom.

Ottosen, R. 2004. Mr. President: The enemy is closer than you might think. In Ottosen, Rune and Nohrstedt, Stig A. (eds.), *U.S. and the others. Global Media Images on "The War on Terror."* Nordicom.

Ottosen, R. 2004. The Norwegian Media Image of the War in Afghanistan: Peacekeeping or Aggression? *Conflict & Communication*, 3(1 & 2). Republished (2005) in Nordicom Review 1.

Ottosen, R. 2007. The Reagans: Fiction, History or Propaganda? In Riegert Kristina (ed.), *Politicotainment. Televisions Take on the Real*. New York: Peter Lang.

Ottosen, R. and Figenschou, T. U. 2007. September 11 in Norwegian Media: Media Images of the Local Threat. In Tomasz Pludowski (ed.), *How the World's News Media Reacted to 9/11*. Spokane: Marquette Books LLC.

Ottosen, R., and Nohrstedt, S. A. 2005. Introduction. In Ottosen, Rune and Nohrstedt, Stig A (eds.), *Global War—Local Views. Media Images of the Iraq War.* Gothenburg: Nordicom.

Ottosen, R., Höijer, B., and Nohrstedt, S. A. 2002. The Kosovo War in the Media—Analysis of a Global Discursive Order, *Conflict & Communication*, 2.

Ottosen, R., and Nohrstedt, S. A. (eds.) 2005. *Global War—Local Views. Media Images of the Iraq War.* Gothenburg: Nordicom.

Ottosen, R., and Nohrstedt, S. A. 2004. *U.S. and the others. Global Media Images on "The War on Terror."* Nordicom.

Peleg, S. 2002. If Words Could Kill: The Demise of Discourse in the Israeli Public Space, *State and Society* (Medina Vehevra), 2(3), pp. 421-444. Haifa University, December. Reprinted (2003). Jerusalem: Academon Books (Hebrew).

Peleg, S. 2007. In Defense of Peace Journalism: A Rejoinder, *Conflict & Ccommunication*, 6(1), October.

Peleg, S. 2003. Disparate and Hostile: The Concept of the "Other"' in the Israeli Society, *Panim*, pp. 23, 37-47, Fall (Hebrew).

Peleg, S. 2003. One's Terrorist is Another's Blockbuster: Political Terrorism in American Versus European Films, *New England Journal of Politics*, 1(1), September.

Peleg, S. 2005. A Palestinian state -yes or no?: Constructing Political Discourse in The Israeli Print News Media: An Experimental Design, *Conflict & Communication*, 3(4), October.

Peleg, S. 2006. Peace Journalism through the Lenses of Conflict Theory: Analysis and Practice, *Conflict & Communication*, 5(2), April. Republished (2007) in Dov Shinar and Wilhelm Kempf (eds.), *Peace Journalism: The State of the Art*. Berlin: Regener.

Peleg, S. 1997. *Spreading the Wrath of God: From Gush Emunim to Rabin Square.* Hakibutz Hameuhad, Tel Aviv (Hebrew).

Peleg, S. 2002. *Zealotry and Vengeance: Quest of a Religious Identity Group.* Lanham MD: Lexington Books.

Peleg, S., and Kempf, W. (eds). (2006). *Fighting Terrorism in the Liberal State: An Integrated Model of Research, Intelligence and International Law.* Amsterdam: IOS-Press.

Projektgruppe Friedensforschung Konstanz (Hrsg.). 2005. *Nachrichtenmedien als Mediatoren von Peace-Building, Demokratisierung und Versöhnung in Nachkriegsgesellschaften.* Berlin: Regener (304S.)

Ross, S. D. 2006. (De) Constructing conflict: A focused review of war and peace journalism, *Conflict & Communication*, 5(2). Republished (2007) in Dov Shinar and Wilhelm Kempf (eds), *Peace Journalism: The State of the Art*. Berlin: Regener Publishing.

Ross, S. D. 2003. Framing of the Palestinian/Israeli conflict in thirteen months of *New York Times* editorials surrounding the attacks of Sept. 11, 2001, *Conflict & Communication*, 2(2).

Ross, S. D. 2003. Images of Irish-Americans: Invisible, inebriated, or irascible. In Paul Martin Lester & S.D. Ross (eds.), *Images that Injure* (2nd ed.), pp. 131-140. Westport, CT: Praeger.

Ross, S. D. 2007. Peace Journalism: Constructive media in a global community, *Global Media Journal: Mediterranean Edition*, 2(2), pp. 33-81, Fall.

Ross, S. D. 2003. Unconscious, ubiquitous frames. In Paul Martin Lester & S.D. Ross (eds.), *Images that Injure* (2nd ed.), pp. 29-34. Westport, CT: Praeger.

Ross, S. D. 2003. Unequal combatants on an uneven media battlefield: Palestine and Israel. In Paul Martin Lester & S.D. Ross (eds.), *Images that Injure* (2nd ed.), pp. 57-64. Westport, CT: Praeger.

Ross, S. D., & Philemon B. 2006. Frame shifts and catastrophic events: The attack of Sept. 11, 2001, and *New York Times's* portrayals of Arafat and Sharon, *Mass Communication & Society,* 9(1), pp. 85-101.

Shinar, D. 2002. Cultural Conflict in the Middle East: The Media as Peacemakers. In E. Gilboa (ed.), *Media and Conflict: Framing Issues, Making Policy, Shaping Opinions.* Ardsley NY: Transnational.

Shinar, D. 2007. Democracy, Development, Peace and Communication: An Overview of their Roles and Interaction, *Global Media Journal: Mediterranean Edition*, 2(1), Spring, pp. 54-62.

Shinar, D. 2005. The Media in Peacemaking: Values and Examples. In U. Lebel. Sede Boqer (eds.), *Security and Communication: The Dynamics of Interrelationship.* Ben Gurion University of the Negev Press (Hebrew).

Shinar, D. 2004. Media peace discourse: Constraints, concepts and building blocks, *Conflict & Communication,* 3(1-2).

Shinar, D. 2007. Peace Journalism: The State of the Art, *Conflict & Communication,* 6(1), April.

Shinar, D. 2003. Peace Process in Cultural Conflict: The Role of the Media, *Conflict & Communication,* 2(1).

Shinar, D. 2004. Tecnicas, narrativas e etica na cobertura das guerras (Techniques, Narratives, and Ethics in the Coverage of War). In S. V. Moreira and A. Bragança (eds.), *Midia, etica e sociedade* (Media, Ethics, and Society). Belo Horizonte, Brazil: Intercom & PUC Minas.

Shinar, D., and Kempf, W. (eds.). 2007. *Peace Journalism. The State of the Art.* Berlin: Regener.

Contributors

Robert A. Hackett is professor of communication at Simon Fraser University, Vancouver, co-director of NewsWatch Canada and co-founder of Canadians for Democratic Media. He has written extensively on journalism, political communication, and media representation. His recent works include Remaking Media: The struggle to democratize public communication (2006, with William Carroll) and Democratizing Global Media: One World, Many Struggles (2005, co-edited with Yuezhi Zhao). Hackett serves on the editorial boards of Journalism Studies and four other journals in the field.

Associate Professor *Jake Lynch* is director of the Centre for Peace and Conflict Studies at the University of Sydney and co-author of Peace Journalism (Hawthorn Press, 2005). Previously he was a professional journalist. He worked as a presenter and reporter for BBC World, a political correspondent for Sky News and as Sydney correspondent for the Independent newspaper.

Lea Mandelzis is a senior lecturer at the School of Communication, Sapir Academic College in Israel. A former professional journalist in Israel, she focuses her research on conflicts, war and peace discourse in the news media. Her work contributes to media monitoring, developing a university peace journalism curriculum, and Keshev, the Organization for the Protection of Democracy in Israel.

Annabel McGoldrick is an experienced international reporter in television and radio, presently for SBS World News Australia. She teaches at the Centre for Peace and Conflict Studies at the University of Sydney and is also a practicing psychotherapist. She is co-author of Peace Journalism (Hawthorn Press, 2005).

Rune Ottosen is professor in journalism at Oslo University College. He has a background as journalist and political scientist and has also he worked as information director and research fellow at the International Peace Research Institute, Oslo (PRIO). He has published several articles and books within the field of press history and war- and peace journalism.

Samuel Peleg is a professor of political science and communication at the School of Communication at Netanya College and a senior lecturer at the Inter-Disciplinary Center (IDC) in Herzliya, Israel. Dr. Peleg is an expert in conflict and conflict-resolution processes and a research fellow at the Stanford Center for International Conflict resolution and negotiation (SCICN). He is completing a book about Dialogue as Conflict Management.

Susan Dente Ross is professor and associate dean at Washington State University, a Fulbright Scholar, and a former journalist and newspaper owner. As the coordinator of the Toda Peace Journalism team, her research contributes to several multi-national projects to reform media practices and develop a peace journalism curriculum.

Birgitta Schroeder is a graduate student in the School of Communication at Simon Fraser University. Her research interests focus on political communication, social movements, international/intercultural conflict communication and media literacy. Her professional experience includes media monitoring/analysis for Greenpeace International and research assistance and data analysis for NewsWatch Canada.

Professor *Dov Shinar* is coordinator of Graduate Studies and head of FAIR MEDIA: Center for the Study of Conflict, Peace and War Coverage in the School of Communication, Netanya Academic College, in Israel. He is professor emeritus at both Concordia University, Montreal, and Ben Gurion University, Israel. His areas of research and publication are international communication, communication and social development, peace journalism and public diplomacy.

Majid Tehranian is senior research fellow and former director of the Toda Institute for Global Peace and Policy Research and adjunct professor at Soak University of America.

For Product Safety Concerns and Information please contact our EU
representative GPSR@taylorandfrancis.com
Taylor & Francis Verlag GmbH, Kaufingerstraße 24, 80331 München, Germany